Comedia/Minority Press Group Series • No 6

The Republic of Letters

Working class writing and local publishing

Paddy Maguire, Roger Mills, Dave Morley,
Rebecca O'Rourke, Sue Shrapnel,
Ken Worpole and Stephen Yeo

Edited by Dave Morley and Ken Worpole

Comedia Publishing Group
9 Poland Street, London W1 3DG. Tel. 01-437 8954

Comedia Publishing Group (formerly Minority Press Group) was set up to investigate and monitor the radical and alternative media in Britain and abroad today. The aim of the project is to provide basic information, investigate problems areas, and to share the experiences of those working within the radical media and to encourage debate about its future development.
For a list of other titles in the Minority Press Group Series, see page 157.

First published in 1982 by Comedia Publishing Group
9 Poland Street, London W1V 3DG. Tel: 01-437 8954

© Comedia Publishing Group and the authors

ISBN 0 906890 12 8 (paperback)
ISBN 0 906890 13 6 (hardback)

Designed by Pat Kahn.
Typeset by Manchester Free Press
Bombay House, 59 Whitworth Street, Manchester M1 3WT (061-228 0976)
Printed in Great Britain by
The Russell Press, 45 Gamble Street, Nottingham NG7 4ET (0602 784505)

Trade distribution by
Southern Distribution, Albion Yard, Balfe Street, London N1
(01-837 1460)
Scottish & Northern Distribution, 4th Floor, 18 Granby Row, Manchester
M13 (061-228 3903)
Scottish & Northern Distribution, 48a Hamilton Place, Edinburgh
EH1 5AX (031-225 4950)

Contents

Starting points

'*Universal empire is the prerogative of the writer... The Republic of Letters is more ancient than monarchy, and of far higher character in the world than the vassal court of Britain.*'
—*Tom Paine*

'I hated school. Everything was so orderly, correct and restricting. Self-expression seemed to be alien to the whole grey, anti-quated building. The male teachers were nothing like my father and the female ones nothing like my mother, or any other relatives, come to that. My lot sounded, and even looked friendlier than these beings. They looked as though they had just been taken out of a showcase. Their tone and accent had an aloofness about it that made it impossible to strike up any sort of relationship whatsoever. We were as remote as shit from sugar.' —Ron Barnes, 'Coronation Cups and Jam Jars'

'*There is a further claim that can be made for the restoration of the teaching of correct English. Attention to the rules of grammar, or care in the choice of words encourages punctiliousness in other matters. That is not just an intellectual conceit. The overthrow of grammar coincided with the acceptance of the equivalent of "creative writing" in social behaviour. As nice points of grammar were mockingly dismissed as pedantic and irrelevant, so was punctiliousness in such matters as honesty, responsibility, property, gratitude, apology and so on.*'
—*John Rae, Headmaster of Westminster School*
in 'The Observer' 7.2.82

Happy Years

In 1946 I married Harry.
Maria our daughter.
Gerrard our son.
Happy years.
Five years ago I had a stroke.
Five months in hospital.
Paralysed down one side
Walking is difficult.
Talking is difficult.
Tip of my tongue.
But the right words won't come out.
In time it'll come.

—Eileen Williamson, 'Tip of My Tongue'

'Whether that is literature, or whether that is not literature, I will not presume to say, but that it explains much and tells much, that is certain.'
—*Virginia Woolf, introduction to 'Life as we have known it'*

'There is no doubt in the minds of the Committee that on a community level the work is of sound value and... a new reading public is responding to this situation. Nevertheless... no recommendation for grant-aid from the Literature budget can be forthcoming. The members were of one voice in judging the examples of literature submitted; they considered the whole corpus of little, if any, solid literary merit...'   —Charles Osborne, Literary Director, Arts Council of Great Britain

'Literature is a place for generosity and affection and hunger for equals – not a prize fight ring. We are increased, confirmed in our medium, roused to do our best, by every good writer, every fine achievement. Would we want one good writer or fine book less? The sense of writers being pitted against each other is bred primarily by the workings of the commercial market place, and by critics lauding one writer at the expense of another while ignoring the existence of nearly all.'
—*Tillie Olsen, 'Silences' p. 174.*

'It is important that we do all we can to increase audiences for today's writers, not that we increase the number of writers. There are already too many writers chasing too few readers. Although the real writer will always emerge without coaxing, it is not so easy to encourage new readers into existence.'
—Charles Osborne, Literary Director, Arts Council

No Dawn in Poplar

When the sun comes up in the morning
rising slowly
the sun comes up
it's the sun coming up.

There's no dawn in Poplar.

—Richard Brown, Tower Hamlets

Hung Up

I've got a theory
That the K.G.B.
are monitoring our phonecalls
(very secretly)
if not,
Last time around,
What was it
Made you sound,
So foreign to me?

—'Voices'

'The Encyclopedia of Article Ideas gives you over ten thousand saleable ideas — which you yourself can actually shape into marketable ideas.' —*Advertisement*

'Which reminds me that the strong minded, practical girl is definitely out of place in these novels, since the creation of terror in the mind of the heroine is a vital element... Having given the requirements for a successful Gothic novel, let us consider the taboos, which are as follows:

1. Any considerable departure from the plot formula.
2. A setting which is entirely matter-of-fact and lacking any air of mystery or danger.
3. A 'Women's Lib' type of heroine.
4. A heroine whose character has undergone neither change nor development by the end of the story.
5. A sad ending.
6. Too-rapid pace, and a completely rational explanation for everything that has happened.
7. Sexual contacts or risque situations.'

—An article on writing Gothic novels in *The Writer* magazine.

'*STORYBUILDER: A brilliant new approach to the step-by-step creation of the modern short story to meet today's editorial needs. Everything you ever wanted to know, from the moment you sit down at your typewriter till you post off your completed story to an editor, told in simple, clear language with no vague generalisations. Choosing your theme. The unique Plot Chart offers you a personal choice from thousands of basic frameworks. Creation – the essential mental process. The secret of the opening paragraph. How to write crisp, natural dialogue...*'
—*Advertisement*

'I was speaking to one of our local pensioners one day, at the beginning of making this book. I happened to bump into her, and I said, "Oh, I can't stay because I'm late. I'm writing a book." And she says to me, "I would like to do that," she said, "but I don't know how to go about it."'
—Joyce Crump, 'The Ups and Downs of Being Born'

'*Adults who are learning to read often say that the easiest pieces to learn to read are the ones which sound most like the way people speak. This helps break down the barrier of print. The language is part of the story. It is often an oral language, alive and central to the atmosphere and feeling.*'   —*Gatehouse leaflet*

'Wednesdays was our day for poetry lesson, and naturally we had to recite what we had learned and the teacher always picked a kid who stammered to recite first: he'd say things like, "Speak up boy, don't mumble, put some life into it, you're not saying 'have a cup of tea'." By the time he'd finished, the kid stammered worse than ever. Then there was Friday afternoons. Before he came it used to be classed as leisure time. We were allowed to bring along our own books and comics to read, but Dean put the kibosh on that. He opened a school library and made us choose our books from it and when we finished a book we had to write an essay on it. I don't think he was trying to interest us in literature; he was probably being his normal sweet self. I remember Billy Jarmyn suffered a lot. He'd picked a dull book by Sir Walter Scott and having a bad memory,when he'd finished his book he'd forgot what he had read and was forced to start again – he was landed with Sir Walter Scott for a whole term! I doubt if he took much interest in books after that.'
—Jim Wolveridge, 'Ain't It Grand'

'*To some people a Union poetry debate may not seem much, yet since last November we have had more readers' letters, more contributions from other unions, than ever before...*'
—*Editorial in TGWU monthly journal, The Record*

'As we arrange courses and study-circles for the working class in Sweden, we find that books written by "ordinary people" (a reference to Centerprise books bought in large quantities) are a lot more interesting than the usual stuff we can get through "educational experts" of various kinds... books about vicars spending their afternoons drinking tea in lovely thatched cottages and that sort of thing...   —From a letter from the Swedish WEA to the Gatehouse project

> Eleven times I tried to write
> another poem for the People's Road
> Five hours within myself
> trains were moving
> signals changed
> night gathered immense wagons
> in a string of stars
> sun shuffled
> shunting dawns
> & I could not write
>
> I had forgotten myself
> in the studied books
> lost my own experience
> in the history of others
> become the old events
> & I could not write
>
> There's learning for you
> The road itself had taught
> to live is to be
> perception first, then memory
>
> I remember these lives within
> from a sense of being
> one with the road
> which book is peopled
> as this twelfth success
> with what I saw when the eyes were mine
>
> —Joe Smythe, Commonword, Manchester

'*But perhaps the real achievement of (this movement) lies in the fact that, over and above making a reality of working class culture, it redefines the "political" in terms of the struggle of individuals to recapture the right to articulate their own situation.*'
—*Mike Poole, Time Out*'

Introduction

The Republic of Letters examines how in recent years working class people, particularly women and black people, have begun to develop new forms of writing, new modes of local, collective publishing, and alternative distribution networks – the elements of a movement which aims to 'disestablish' literature, making writing a popular form of expression for all people rather than the preserve of a metropolitan or privileged elite.

Many of the people involved in these initiatives – in adult education and literacy classes, in community publishing projects, in writers' groups and local history workshops – came together in 1976 to form the Federation of Worker Writers & Community Publishers. Poetry, stories, autobiographies are all now being produced outside the established field of 'Literature' and the market economies of commercial publishing.

The book looks critically at the policies of the Labour and trade union movements towards the Arts, particularly writing and publishing, and at the dismissive response which the Arts Council has made to this lifely and growing phenomenon.

The Republic of Letters examines the problems as well as the very real successes of the recent movement, and discusses possible lines of development for the future. We hope it will be helpful to those people already active in the writing and community publishing movement, particularly those in groups who are members of the Federation of Worker Writers & Community Publishers, but also to those active outside this federation.

This book addresses a number of questions concerning all writers and readers – questions of literature and literacy – and in particular questions about the way these matters are dealt with in schools and other educational institutions. The book speaks also to trade unionists and socialists who believe that the broad labour movement cannot restrict its vision to economic equality alone, but who believe that all forms of cultural production are equally the right of working people. It is a book of analysis but also we hope of genuine encouragement.

Early days and community politics

In 1976 representatives of eight groups engaged in the publishing of local histories, poetry and autobiographies met for a weekend of discussion at the Centerprise bookshop and cultural centre in London. It was here that the Federation of Worker Writers and Community Publishers was born.

The title is wordy and loose yet its terms are important. A Federation rather than other forms of organisation, to keep the autonomy of the member groups. Worker writers, to register the fact that the working class, the majority of the population, are still, in Tillie Olsen's words, 'marginal to the culture'. Community Publishers, because almost all of the member groups have a local base and local boundaries, and the intention to continue together in their future work.

This book is about the work and development of these groups and their Federation, about the work of allied groupings who are not members, and about the issues in politics and culture raised by these practices, the sometimes unresolved problems of this work. It is written by people active in this movement, aware that we have not been able to refer everything back to our various, argumentative, active, vital and changing groups, or even fully to each other. It's one road through a complicated patch of ground.

The oldest of the groups meeting in February 1976 went back only five years but, as projects sprang up in different towns and cities, they had begun to visit each other, correspond and exchange ideas and experience. A later section will examine the forerunners and origins of this activity, but we need to say here why it was that parallel developments of this kind had come about in different places within a few years of each other.

During the 1960's political and social activity turned away from the electoral, national and bureaucratic towards the local, campaigning, direct action, sectional and self-organised. Groups of working class people, finding that no formal structure dealt adequately with needs and issues as they felt them, began to represent themselves. They took direct action in the form of rent-strikes, the playgroup and nursery movement, squatting, housing and tenants' co-ops, free schools, the creation of local and accessible print and resources centres. And, growing out of face-to-face politics but rapidly transcending the local, there grew black politics and the women's liberation movement.

The fact that these various, deeply resistant and creative movements were perjoratively categorised 'community politics', and exploited by local and national politicians and their policies, points to one of the problems of basing activity in the 'local'. Locality is not a power base; it may not even define common interests. It can be an assertive badge of class; but it can be a divisive screen to separate people from wider allegiancies and produce a false togetherness. We may only begin to articulate the values of a neighbourhood as it, and they, are dismantled. But, at its best, the local in politics stands for testing policies and actions by their impact on people's day-to-day life and development – as with the group in Liverpool who, when commissioned to contribute to a Lord Mayor's Enquiry into Crime and Vandalism in the Inner City, produced a paper called 'We Live Here'.

Local communications

Local battles need local communications. The booklet, *Here is the Other News*, in this series, is an excellent account of the development of alternative and community presses. People seized hold of the idea that the new off-set lithography was a form of printing that was more amenable to local control and local participation. Photographic plate-making meant that typing; drawings and half-tone photographs could be reproduced directly. This made design and layout a possibility for anybody. Gradually the use of this accessible form of printing moved from the campaigning and critical – the broadsheet, the leaflet, the strike bulletin, the exposing community paper – to reproduction of writing in forms which we are used to calling literature. (This is not an apology; we will argue later that such writings are not third-class literature but a challenge to the category of Literature). And, from the start, this did not mean a diversion from campaigning writing to something tame and bland. Literature threatens and disturbs too. *Stepney Words* was published in 1971, a collection of poems by school children. Their critical view of their world in print led to the suspension from his post at the school of its editor, Chris Searle, and a demonstration by the young contributors and their parents for his reinstatement.

Why publishing?

In the same month, just two miles up the road, the Centerprise bookshop and cultural centre was opened, one of the first of the alternative and community bookshops which came to be of great value to the local publishing movement. They are sales points, sometimes mail order distributors, places where people bring writing to be looked at, sometimes publishers or supporters of publishing. They are physical bases for this movement of self-development and self-organisation. (See, for example, *Rolling Our Own* in this series, for an account of the relationship between Grass Roots Bookshop in Manchester, and the project on Law and Sexuality.)

Centerprise began publishing with the writing of young people – their educational and cultural needs – in mind. (We will have more to say later about the place of this work in educational practice). But, in Hackney as everywhere, it became clear that, against the odds, many people were writing who had no educational reasons and little outside encouragement for doing so.

Once it became known that Centerprise published books written by local people, a great deal of material began to come in. In the main it was either small collections of poetry, or autobiographies, often just childhood recollections. The initial criteria for deciding what to publish were simple. Given limited resources and so much material we decided that whatever we published had to be clearly written and understandable to a wide cross-section of people; it must honestly reflect and allow the reader to understand the writers' experiences. We would also look for writing that embodied good description and critical thinking, and we would give priority to local people who had not had any opportunities for further education...

As it turned out, few manuscripts caused severe editorial difficulties. What was nice was the way in which one piece in print would inspire other people to put pen to paper. We got poems in response to poems we had already published, people confirming or taking issue with historical incidents in published autobiographies. There was an extraordinarily high level of response and feedback to the books.   —*Writing*, p.38.

Another common strand of development was the move from local issues into recording local history, either as memoirs by a single person or as an assembly of many. Campaigns over the quality of life in an area found natural allies in the recovery and recording of its past, not out of any simple illusions about the good old days, but because the life of the past represented the investment of human energy that was to be cherished and allowed to address itself to new needs.

This was the origin of QueenSpark Books:

The newspaper (QueenSpark) started in December 1972... It grew from a fierce campaign to stop Brighton Council turning a historic building in a park (The Royal Spa) into a casino, and to get a nursery school, day nursery and park centre instead. As a matter of policy the paper is sold almost entirely door-to-door. A thousand copies of our first QueenSpark Book (Albert Paul's *Poverty, Hardship But Happiness*) also sold in less than a month in this way. The selling system involves area contacts and some 40 individual street sellers. With the paper goes a duplicated slip for letters and comments.

... The development from newspaper to book publishing came by way of a historical feature in the paper called *Sparchives*. This was based on a series of interviews, mostly researched by Molly Morley... The *Sparchives* feature led Albert Paul to bring his book to *QueenSpark*. He had sat down to write it one evening per week over several months, when his wife had an evening out. A production team was formed, and since then we have tried to have separate teams on each book. More recently we have had book evenings occasionally to read aloud, plan and talk. —*Writing*, pp.151, 154, 157.

There were some immediate forerunners of this way of looking at history – important because they helped people to recognise and shape what was happening. The rare appearance on BBC radio of work like Ewan MacColl and Charles Parker's 'Radio Ballads' in the 50's and early 60's (*Ballad of John Axon, Singing the Fishing, The Big Hewer,* etc) had go many people excited about using tape to record the wealth of history, reflection, story, jokes and myth that lives in people's talk. The Ruskin College History Workshops, which originated amongst tutors and students in the mid-sixties, created the basis for a new kind of popular history. They encouraged original research by the worker-students themselves, about the places they came from, the lives and occupations of their families, histories of their trade or union, and so opened up the consideration of people's lived historical experience as a counter to the narrowness of text-book history. The phrase that most neatly describes this approach, 'Dig where you stand', comes though, not from Ruskin, but from the title of Sven Lindquist's Swedish handbook on researching your workplace.

The cassette tape-recorder was a technical development which lent itself to these uses as readily as litho printing to shared control of print. Oral and written history go together to make many of the Federation books. This is what Greg Wilkinson wrote about the Partington Lifetimes series:

We began meeting and recording early in 1974. To begin with it was mostly just one person or a couple, with me as a pretty traditional interviewer. We started like this because the authors were not sure how many people they could talk to. I'd get some written notes from them before we met, and base my questioning on those. Simple questions mainly, like 'How did that happen?' 'What then?' 'How did you feel about it?' and 'Why?' These sessions were taped and transcribed, and two copies of the transcripts given to the speakers − one for themselves, one for anybody else in the group that they wanted to show. It was soon clear that everyone was willing for everyone to see their transcripts, so we took to duplicating them and distributing them around. As people got less shy and more involved, we moved into larger groups. Other people began asking the questions, freeing me to be more myself. One person began writing rather than talking − she said she couldn't get a word in with her husband around. And most people wrote some part, which could then be picked up in live discussion. We found that reading aloud brought a much more active response than leaving people to read the duplicated versions to themselves.

—*Writing*, pp.114-115.

New ways to write

This description leads to one further basic characteristic of the Federation's member groups: the workshop group. Spending a substantial part of its time in face-to-face meetings is the usual way they work either at history or at writing. This doesn't necessarily mean writing during group meetings (though it's not unknown). It does mean a commitment to using the group as the first readership or audience for work, and as the body that decides about editing, shaping, public reading or publication. One last description of a group that was in the Federation from the beginning:

The Scotland Road Writers' Workshop was born in the autumn of 1973. Its founders included an out-of-work electrician, a dock-gate man, a fireman, an O-level dropout, a militant feminist − all working-class people − and a university lecturer in literature. Since then over fifty people have been part of the workshop at some time or another and attendance at weekly sessions has come to average a creditable thirteen.

The initial aim was simply to try to find some of the imaginative talent we know to exist in Britain's poor and exploited inner city areas. For this reason the founders stressed that the workshop was not concerned with grammar or fine writing but with finding words for working class ideas and experiences and feelings.

That is what the workshop has done. Within the first few months its members produced not only recollections and pieces about conditions in their area but imaginative work – poems, short stories, plays. And these have not been passing flashes. Production has been steady and expanding. Today members of the group are moving towards matching words to music in the attempt to create popular songs with a social content. Another branch of activity has been the use of tape to record accounts of recent working class struggles – rent strikes and tenants' election campaign for instance. —*Writing*, p.168.

These were the practices of some of the early groups involved in the Federation. We include here a piece of writing from Centerprise (Vivian Usherwood), from QueenSpark (Molly Morley) and from Scotland Rd (Jimmy McGovern).

The sun glitters as you look up

The sun glitters, is shining bright!
The sky is blue!
The clouds are no longer there:
It glitters as I look up!
Bright it is, bright as my sister's face:
The sun looks like a face without a body,
Just round, with a nose and two eyes.
If only that beautiful face would come down –
It will be mine,
And I shall shine with it.
As dim as I am now I will be brighter,
Even brighter than the sun itself.
So it shall be,
And I shall be as dim as ever,
For it shall stay there for many years to come.

—from *Vivian Usherwood: Poems*

Carlton Hill – when we were young

An area of dealers and totters: you would see them sorting their rags, and then the mums would come to find clothing and other useful items for a few pennies. There was more profit in this than when it was all weighed up for the trade. Some women would buy flour-bags: these, by cutting head and arm holes, would make children's frocks, or opened up become sheets. People were borrowing from one another – tea, sugar, anything – all the time. Mrs Calder, at the William St. corner shop, used to help people by selling them a farthingworth of tea and ha'porths of sugar and milk. A packet of tea could be bought for 1d in those days. Street doors ever open, a hungry child might wander in and be asked, 'Haven't you had any dinner' and answer, 'No, I ain't 'ad nothin'.' The expected, 'here y'are then, have some of this', was a moment of joy! As families grew large this often meant moving house. Those of eleven children might also have relatives and grandparents nearby. Children called their neighbours aunts and uncles too. Although a rough area, there was no necessity for locked doors. Thieves lived there but never stole in their own neighbourhood. Had one dared, the wrath of a whole community would have sealed his fate! Friday nights were very tough! A man recalls seeing two women fighting bare down to their waists, and they each had every bit of clothing torn off them! The men just stood around. When one woman had had enough her husband pulled her out of the gutter by her hair! The police would patrol Carlton Hill 'four-handed' (four at a time). There was the night in Carlton Court when about five policemen were actually knocked out by women – with fire-tongs and pokers! Their menfolk, whom the police were after, had already got clean away!

—*Molly Morley, Sparchives*

The day of the rat

I remember the day we found the rat in Billy Carey's lobby. The rat was grey and wet and it was moving its feet a lot and scratching the floor but it wasn't getting very far. Black stuff was coming out of its nose.

Jimmy Murphy went to Grammar School so we sent to his house for a ruler to measure the rat. It was six inches long, but its tail measured seven inches, and Jack O'Reilly said that if it had been another five inches, it would have been half a yard long. Five inches didn't seem a lot so we always afterwards described the rat as half a yard long. It wasn't a big lie and I always counted it in on Fridays, at Confession!

None of us would pick up the rat. Gerry Rowan was best at picking up because he could pick up a cockroach. I was second best, because I could pick up wood lice, but a rat was something else. It was a hundred times worse than a centipede (Gerry Rowan said) even more worse than an earwig, which could run up your sleeve and eat your ear drum away. In the end, we got some sticks and poked them at the rat. It's funny, you know. We were in Billy Carey's lobby so he ought to have been in charge. Gerry Rowan said that Billy ought to charge our mates for having a look, but Billy didn't want to. He was scared of the rat and said that if it had been found in somebody else's lobby, he would have enjoyed himself torturing it, but he didn't like the rat in his own lobby. He said that he was going upstairs to tell his old feller.

Billy's old man worked nights in the bakehouse in Rose Lane. Billy's mam used to say that she was proud of her husband working 84 hours a week on nights to keep her and the kids, and my mam used to say that my old man didn't know there were 84 hours in a week! In any case, my mam said, Billy's mam was on the game.

We heard Billy's old man fizzing away upstairs until he could get the words out, and then he gave Billy a belt which we all felt. When his old man came down the stairs, we were scared stiff because he had only a shirt on and he was scratching his balls and we knew that he wasn't expecting anybody to be in the lobby. We all spewed it before he could get the words out and the next time we saw him, he was coming out the house with his clothes on.

We watched him cross over the street and pick up a brick and then he went back to the lobby and hit the rat with the brick, and all the black stuff splashed over his face. Then he put the rat in his pocket and marched off down the street. Billy's mam come out and folded her arms and waited for the neighbours to come out too.

We knew that Billy's old feller was going to see the Snotty Bitch and we had to trot to keep up with him. When we got there, Billy's dad was in the queue. The Snotty Bitch was going on about points again and then she offered this woman a flat in Kirkby and then when the old woman kept on asking for a house, the Snotty Bitch started to tap her pencil and look sideways at her mate, like she always did. Then another woman came up and the Snotty Bitch soon started tapping her pencil again and looking sideways at her mate. We thought we'd have to wait about two hours for Billy's dad's turn when, all of a sudden, he just marched up to the counter. The Snotty Bitch asked him his present address and Billy's dad tried to get the words out but he couldn't. He was banging his fists against his legs but he still couldn't say anything and all the time, the people behind him in the queue were shouting 'Frigging cheek', and all that kind of thing. The Snotty Bitch started to tap her pencil and look sideways and then Billy's old feller let out a roar and started crying and threw the rat over the rail.

She screamed but at first, she didn't know it was a rat and then when she saw that it was a rat, she just gurgled and fell forward and her face smacked against the rat and she lay there for about five minutes.

Then these two geezers came out the office and took her away and they phoned the Police and the Ambulance, and then they took Billy's dad inside and told him to pull himself together because he couldn't stop crying. I am glad Billy wasn't there.

Four days after this happened, Billy's mam got the offer of a new house in Cantril Farm and they took it. We all kept looking in the *Liverpool Echo,* for a report of what had happened but we didn't see anything. My dad, who is very clever and uses a lot of big words, said that the *Echo* wouldn't report it because of the implications. Implications must be very important because all that week, there were lists of the names of the people who had been fined for not having a telly licence, and a big picture of a man who had worked at the same job for fifty years, but there wasn't even a mention of Billy's dad.

—*Jimmy McGovern*

So you want to be a writer...

We know the talent is there, we know it comes up against (Tillie Olsen's phrase again) 'complex odds' in seeking outlets, so we need to organise in order that these and routes for development exist. Before this, what was there for working-class writers? There was the chance, for a very few, of becoming one of those who are taken up and who make it as novelist, playwright, TV dramatist, very very rarely poet. (We don't think it's appropriate to use the language of cream naturally rising; we know how many obstacles there are to some cream even forming. We know, too, that the market has an appetite for particular kinds of success, but it needs them to be singular. It would be no use to the book trade if every Oxfordshire village produced a Pam Ayres, let alone a crop of women writing poems which fitted less easily within the frame of light entertainment).

There was the less class-bound but highly competitive field of lyric writing for rock music. There were less ambitious outlets such as the historical anecdote in the local paper. There were short stories which some newspapers and more magazines would take (provided these fulfilled the literary norms in which books and courses offered to train you) though most now will only accept work from literary agents.

There was the £5 (1981 prices) for a published letter to a magazine. There was the deadly expensive and ineffective trap of vanity publishing, in which you pay for a small number of copies of your work to be printed (and often hardly distributed at all). This didn't even get you a readership!

It's reasonable to want people to read what you write; but even if you manage to write it (and it should not be necessary to go on at great length about the material obstacles of time, overcrowding, fatigue, anxiety, other priorities; also the cultural problem of underrating yourself; the lack of acceptability of what you are capable of or want to write; language snobbery, and more serious oppression of your language and thought; disbelief by the gate-keepers of the published culture; the tourist approach to poverty and working class life), what chance is there that you will find anyone to whom you can show your work in the expectation that it will be read, understood, supported, answered, propogated and built into culture, without being in some measure stolen from you and from the world that gave rise to it? That is the challenge. This network of groups is part of a response. They have not been able to meet the equally reasonable hope that work done and published should be paid for. But this has deterred very few people; it seems that the desire for readership comes first.

We remain locally organised and federated because this seems one way of continuing to work together and share and develop skills, rather than to pass work over to others who will edit, illustrate, package and market it in a way that the writer cannot control.

However, this decision alone does not guarantee the growth of organic working-class cultural organisations. Some of the groups in the Federation have grown up in areas where most of the residents share a class background, an occupational tradition and a strongly established, sometimes relatively closed way of life. Yet, even here, the development has rarely been without the participation of someone in an educational or 'community' job, or of politically committed incomers (often no easier to deal with in cultural politics than in a Labour Party Ward).

Most of the groups are based in socially mixed areas, or reflect the fact that the break-up of the pre-1939 rigidity and hardship is still very real to many people; they have been discouraged from recognising class as a reality in their new conditions of living and working. Even member groups that have started sure of their base and identity have changed.

Further, in looking at class *cultural* oppression, we have had to confront its overlaps and entanglements with the oppression of black people. Despite the hard work and self-criticism of people writing now we have had to face the fact that white working class traditions have contributed to these oppressions. The author of a

Federation book, a skilled working class man, may be dismissive of the language used in another piece by a West Indian hairdresser. He may also record the weight of the past on women, as in Terence Monaghan's recollection of Tyneside life:

There's no doubt about it, men in that generation were the kingpin of the house. Other people cleaned their shoes. They had a special seat. Nobody dare sit in their seat. This kind of thing. My wife's father, nobody dared pass him in case their shadow went on his newspaper... They were tyrants really in their own way.

Making a Federation

The constitution of the FWWCP, worked out shortly after the founding meeting, chose an inclusive, even vague, form of words when it referred to 'writing produced within the working class and socialist movement or in support of... working class activity and self-expression'. But there is disagreement about emphases. One Annual Meeting included a contentious workshop on 'Working class or Socialist?', insisting that we might have to make a choice. And, apart from the fact that feminist groups would not necessarily see the Federation as serving their interests, it isn't always obvious from the other side either that their aims are the same, and issue 25 of *Voices* prints an argument against admission of a feminist group to the Federation. (*Voices* is a quarterly magazine, originally organised from Manchester now acts as an anthology for the whole Federation.)

There has also been discussion, and different decisions made in different groups, about the role of 'middle-class managers' – those of us who have been involved as educators, bookshop or publishing workers, sometimes servicers of the group's work, paid or unpaid. Like for example, most of those who have met to produce this book.

Some groups hold that these can threaten and inhibit working class writers (by their position, not by behaving badly), or have found it hard to create structures that oblige the 'professionals' to share their skill and confidence so that the group can go on without them.

It should be said also that some of those same 'middle-class managers' have found by working with their local groups an inspiration and incentive to write that they had not experienced before.

The arguments will continue. What is important though, and what represents the opening up of an area formerly closed to working class people is that there are now groups, networks and practices directed to a local history which is also a people's history, and local writing that does not seek to model itself on the prize-winning, official culture. Local groups have existed before — and they have no doubt included working class members. But such groups have never allowed for the possibility that the experience of being exploited could produce a valid and vital view of history. Consequently they have been of no use to the majority of people. Nor have they existed in places where Federation groups now thrive; it was believed that nobody would be interested. The opposite is now proved to be the case. With interest and encouraged together with publication and distribution of their writings, these groups are thriving and growing in number.

Structure and activities

Since that founding meeting in 1976, more local groups have applied to join the Federation each year; today the number of affiliated groups stands at 24. Between them they have achieved sales of well over a half million copies of their publications. Some have had the support (never more than part-time) of paid workers, who may work for a multi-purpose project like Centerprise, THAP or the Peckham Bookplace, or who may be tutors for the WEA or University Extra-Mural Departments. Many carry on with no paid work put in at all; some are specifically concerned with making a place for the writing of those working class adults who are students of literacy. No two groups are alike, for all have different histories and origins.

Yet at some point each member group has found it necessary to formalise itself in order that it can apply for grants, agree on a corresponding address and, of course, apply to join the Federation. This is a moment that many find difficult because it means a change from an informal association of people who write into a group with a business agenda at each meeting and the requirement, if not to elect officers, at least to apportion the working responsibilities. Often this seems a diversion from the main purpose — to talk about writing and to listen to the latest taped interview — but if the group is to have a relationship with the wider movement then the business has to be done. One of the most complex initiation ceremonies is the opening of a corporate bank account in the name of the group — 'Hereafter with regard to the aforesaid rules and regulations excluding such as may have been deemed inappropriate to such offices and executees as are deemed so within the conditions of paragraph 3, sub section 1, *unless* the aforesaid rules and regu-lations...'. It is precisely this kind of language wielded like a heavy baton over popular organisation within our society that we struggle against.

To become members of the Federation, a group contacts the Executive Committee (a body of seven elected members voted to take account of regional representation and a balance of women and men), which then asks the Federation members to visit the applicant and report back. If their report is favourable and accepted by the committee the group can be taken into provisional membership until the next Annual General Meeting, at which its acceptance must be confirmed by all groups present. The idea of scrutinising groups at all has come under attack even though it has rarely led to refusals. One such refusal came about because the application was made by a paid worker rather than by the group members themselves. The main criterion used in deciding whether or not to accept groups into the Federation is whether they are genuinely self-organising and not encouraged into being and still controlled externally within some kind of community development or education programme. Another requirement is that they should have published, or be well on the way to publishing, including duplicated magazines.

Festival of people's literature

Worker Writers gathered this month at Nottingham University for what you might say was a cross between the Oscar awards and a TUC conference.

Some 120 people representing 24 local groups attended the fifth annual general meeting and festival of the Federation of Worker Writers and Community Publishers.

The weekend was a mixture of serious business meetings, discussion groups on various aspects of writing and publishing, and a reading of work by the writers themselves.

The Federation is what it says it is, a national organisation for the promotion and encouragement of working-class writing through writers' workshops and local publishing initiatives.

One of the most important functions of its annual get-together is to allow working-class writers from different towns and cities to meet, exchange experiences and listen to each other's work.

That way lies the development of various new forms of writing and new kinds of writing aesthetics.

A number of people brought their families along with them for the weekend. There were probably slightly more women than men.

On the Saturday morning there were three workshops: the first, a discussion of the editorial policy of the Federation's quarterly magazine

'Voices', which was lively and combative.

Agitprop or 'heroic' verse was increasingly felt to be inappropriate to modern political conditions and the 'politics of the personal.'

The second workshop concerned questions of payment for writing, within the Federation and more obviously in connection with the established media.

The third was for those involved in the forthcoming trip by six writers from Federation groups to the USA at the invitation of the American worker-writers' movement.

The AGM was held on Saturday afternoon. Everyone agreed that it had been a very successful year with the movement growing stronger and stronger.

Highly protracted negotiations with the Arts Council literature panel seemed about to produce a modest one-year scheme for a full-time development worker.

Two new member groups were admitted at the AGM: 'Women and Work' from Birmingham and the Northern College Writers' Workshop – Northern College is a full-time college for people involved in the working-class and labour movement.

The Federation continues to live a precarious financial life: the Gulbenkian Foundation, which has funded a worker for two years, has ended its funding with a supplementary grant which helped toward the cost of the AGM.

An appeal is being circulated to sympathisers for subscriptions to the work of the Federation which can be contacted at 136 Kingsland High St., London, E8.

Late Saturday afternoon workshops dealt with basic book production, relationships between the Federation and other cultural and political organisations and a workshop on women writers in the Federation.

It is Federation policy that women-only workshops and black writers' workshops are automatically eligible for Federation membership as they represent specific sections of the community which have been particularly repressed culturally and linguistically.

The evening reading was a packed and tumultuous affair. Everyone crowded into a large room above the bar and for nearly four hours listened as people from all over the country sang songs, read poems, short plays and stories.

An endless succession of women and men, black people and white, bounced up to the microphone, battled with the feedback and read from the work they had written.

During the reading a collection was taken for the burnt out bookshop in Birmingham and £30 was raised. A party followed the reading.

Sunday morning saw a large bookfair where member groups displayed their publications, talked to each other and sold books.

Member groups between them have now sold well over half a million publications nationally through a form of publishing that involves completely new forms of social relationship between writers, publishing initiatives and readers.

There were also two workshops: one was an account by the Hut Writers, Bristol, of how they run their workshop and the other tackled the complicated and vexed question of 'Working Class Writers/Middle Class Managers?'

Festivals and annual meetings such as these re-affirm our belief that in the past too many voices have been stifled or silenced by the education system and commercial forms of publishing.

We aim to create a living, non-competitive popular history and literature. By the people, for the people.

—*FWWCP Press Release*, April 1981

The Annual General Meeting is turning into an important occasion – part debate, part festival, part business meeting. Up to 120 people meet together, many with children, for a residential weekend whose high spot is always the Saturday night reading. But as well as this, and a variety of workshops, the meeting elects an Executive Committee and officers, and looks at the Federation finances.

Finance

Once you have decided to set up a national network, you need money – even if it's only for correspondence and travel. The AGMs cost more than could possibly be provided by most of the participants (weekend residential costs run around £30 a head, in addition to travel). In the past money has also been needed for specific projects: *Writing* the collection of work from all the groups published in 1978; a mounted and laminated Exhibition which has toured widely since 1979; a recent tour in the United States by six writers from different groups (which derived from our international links with people pursuing similar aims and activities). And the Federation soon decided that, if it was to have the capacity to develop its members' work to the fullest possible extent, it needed a paid co-ordinator.

These needs have been met, or not met, in various ways. Many member groups register with the national or local Poetry Secretariat, so can claim subsidy when they give public readings on their own or each other's ground (often the only way of paying for travel). Member groups pay a small subscription for basic organisational costs, and the better-heeled members and friends are encouraged to make out standing orders. The Gulbenkian Foundation gave a grant which paid for a national co-ordinator's pay and costs for two years (1979 and 1980), and for the cost of Executive and other meetings. (Executive Committee meetings are open to all members.) The Arts Council of Great Britain gave a grant to publish *Writing,* then refused for two years to support the continuation of what the Gulbenkian grant had paid for. They have now agreed to pay for a temporary part-time co-ordinator, and to contribute to travel costs. The Gulbenkian Foundation has recently advanced the costs of a Publications List. Like all radical groups seeking funding from charitable trusts and State bodies, we have found the process full of comedy, frustration and enlightenment; its detailed history will be discussed later. We have not received (or sought directly) substantial backing from the organised labour movement, though they have supported our pressure on the Arts Council.

Meanwhile, since the full-time co-ordinator's post came to an end, more work has fallen on members and the Executive. One most important development has been to publicise and distribute members' books by maintaining two stocks of all publications – currently, one in Manchester and one in London – for reference and to supply bookstalls and local buyers.

The issue of distribution, the importance of what method to choose and the impact this has on the feedback, control, pricing and availability of books, will be discussed later.

Disestablishing literature

Why not, simply, the truth?

By becoming a Federation – by coming into association with each other, sharing and looking at the body of work we have produced between us, making space to reflect on what we do and to bring together our separate reflections – we have put ourselves in a position to challenge Literature as it is dominantly defined. It is a two-fold challenge: we claim both that we are already producing literature, that our books are full and excellent examples of it, rather than provisional statements until we learn the refinements of Craft or Art; and we claim also that our practices are on a collision course with Literature.

This chapter will try to back up and explain both these statements. The challenges, at one level, are made whether we articulate them or not: it's the perception of others that to organise in the way we do around literature is threatening or against the nature of the art. But we are also making these challenges consciously as we reflect on how these books are made, on how they and the activities which surround them are limited by what goes on elsewhere in the culture.

This is a long road from where many of us started, which may have more to do with the question Doris Lessing voices through Anna, the central character of *The Golden Notebook* (1962). This is Anna – reflecting on her first novel:

... now what interests me is precisely this – why did I not write an account of what had happened, instead of shaping a 'story' which had nothing to do with the material that fuelled it. Of course, the straight, simple, formless account would not have been a 'novel' and would not have got published, but I was genuinely not interested in 'being a writer' or even in making money. I am not now talking of that game writers play with themselves when writing, the psychological game – that written incident came from that real incident, that character was transposed from that one in life, this relationship was the psychological twin of that. I am simply asking myself: Why a story at all – not that it was a bad story, or untrue, or that it debased anything. Why not, simply, the truth?

What a question to ask! – at a time when we are all caught up in ideas about how different the proceedings are in each separate head, and when we dread the notion of a public 'truth' as totalitarian. And what a question to ask in relation to literature, which since its beginnings has juggled event, experience and artifice.

Private and public

And yet so many people are drawn to write out of a sense of an unheard truth (our truth, my truth, social and personal), and of the violence done in the gap between our ideas and what goes on in the world. This gap has become a chasm into which the majority of us fall or get pushed, with 'silent', 'apathetic', 'quite happy with the way things are', 'depressed', 'housebound', 'in need of a break', or 'unfortunately I cannot sign my name' wrapped round our necks.

In this situation 'my life' becomes private – of no possible interest to anyone else. Federation groups have found this to be the first obstacle and the first achievement. How can memories written for a grandchild, with all the directness of that most private of forms – the letter – telling *him* all kinds of truths which *he*. with *his* college training and cars, is utterly ignorant of, how can such memories be of interest to anyone else? How *can* they be worth publishing? The books between private private and public often work on this rich border-line. They have the sharpness, the confidence, and the varieties of register which characterise letters, rather than 'writing' which has got itself up, dressed for public display. They came into being without a public in mind, or rather without a public of the kind implied by purchase through the market.

In favourable circumstances, when these things are published, the intensity of response is such that other forms of writing become possible. Not only do rival memories rush in, with one Federation book leading directly to another (in Brighton the sequence is particular clear, with Albert Paul stimulating Daisy Noakes, Daisy stimulating Bert Healey and so on), but also having one book published leads directly into another by the same author. This isn't automatic: it needs ways of making the response known, of bringing people together, and of making further opportunities to write open and really possible – in other words it needs organisation, and organisation of a kind directed carefully to these ends.

The books are full of direct address: 'let me tell you a story...' and 'as I was saying'. But 'direct' doesn't mean 'naive'. There is no simple relationship between the 'truth' and the telling, and everyone who tries it finds that 'telling' immediately becomes 'making' — becomes art. The books reflect on the making of the tale even as it is being told.

And the tale has often been made in many different ways — the extreme example being the Manchester, seven volume, *Lifetimes* series which contains recorded conversations, direct writing, editorial reflection, and individually-made tapes.This project is full of courageous self-consciousness: painful, quickening, embarrassing in different moments, and much more available for criticism in constructive ways than has yet been taken advantage of.

These books often ignore time, and linear, logical sequence. They weave in and out of moments, family lives, funny stories, connected by their significance for the teller rather than by their succession in a particular 'career', or correct, seamless narrative.

My father is on the broad side and tall side. My father was a hard working man and he had a lot of money. He was not fat or thin... His age was about thirty years when he died, he had a good reputation, he is a married man. When he was in hospital I went to see him every Sunday afternoon. I asked him how he was going on, he told me he was getting a lot better. My father was very kind to me and gave me and my cousins cigarette cards. He likes doing woodwork, my father, for me, and he likes a little game of cards now and then; or a game of darts. He chops wood and saws the planks and he is a handsome man but he is dead. He worked at the rubber works before he died. (9 year old boy)
    Teacher's comment: 'Tenses. You keep mixing past and present'.
—*Jackson, English Versus Examinations, 1965.*

Indeed, the autobiograhpical accent in Federation work is specifically not about careers or good works, either in the *Men, Movements and Myself* labour autobiographical genre or in the spiritual, confessional, Puritan one. They move easily between accurate memory, triggered often by a product name (maybe of an old patent medicine) or a badge, a street — and direct speech, but direct speech re-created in a skilful literary way by authors who were not there to hear it. (The best example, and a fine book in *any* company, is Ron Barnes' *Coronation Cups and Jam Jars.*) They deal with things which are the common subject of talk but not often of writing, such as hospital operations, school violence (by the teachers rather than the taught), humiliations mixed with pride in domestic and factory work, the details of (mostly women's) work towards survival at times (recent times) when survival has been a very creative, co-operative and labour-intensive achievement.

The functions of writing

The possibility of writing like this, and of letting the writing out, with all the risks that involves, is there because it is a movement back into social life and not out of it. Writing is openly functional. That is to say, the books often tell how writing has enabled the author to associate and communicate a story in alliance with a known group of persons or community, rather than telling how success has enabled further exile in the haven at the top of the house where the lonely writer sits or the haven overseas where the poor-rich writer avoids his tax. *The Ups and Downs of Being Born* by Joyce Crump is only 42 pages long and 75p, so there is no point in proving its quickening pleasures here, beyond a few words at its beginning:

'In this book', the introduction says,

I have tried to tell you about my real life. It's not been easy to tell, because remembering is not easy. There is a lot even now that I've left out. And, like a lot of people, I find writing hard to do on my own. If it hadn't been for the tape recorder, this book would never have been written. I wrote it by talking with Jane, and by making visits with Caroline. Maggie, Jane and Ian typed it all out. Then I worked with my friends at the Union Place Resource Centre to design and print the book.

Life hasn't been easy, and it isn't easy today. During the winter we were working on the book, both my daughter and my grand-daughter were very ill. We still live under difficult conditions.

The Neighbourhood Council and local activities take up a lot of my time. It means a lot to me, and I want to say thank you to them for helping me to be involved in the community. They've stopped me from becoming a hermit. They've helped me to be in touch with other people.

Much of the writing has been historical, based on memory, experience, and investivation. But this has not meant that the books have lost the qualities of clarity, warmth and accessibility. The word is not 'immediate', because as we have already said, the awareness and use of the medium is swift to develop and often skilful; but they are readable in a way that the dominant forms of history-writing, including socialist work intending to be popular, rarely are.

In describing and celebrating what we do we have constantly been returning it to its context, considering it in the light of what it has done for others, or for the writers, as part of their lives; we haven't considered texts as things on their own. Does this play into the hands of those who put down the work as therapeutic, 'community writing', if not pre-literate (although sometimes it is that), then certainly pre-literature? We would prefer to stress the positives behind these negatives: better therapeutic than disabling, better community writing than writers in isolation, better the contributions from all than the inaccessible pinnacles of 'talent'. But we would also claim that this body of work, this 'school' of writing, has its own characteristics, excellences and shortcomings, and is beginning to develop its own standards. Among these is the conviction that work which may be, from some people's point of view, not so good as other work, is essential to the growth of the best, and that it should not be removed from view, as Criticism does to work falling outside the great literary tradition. Practically this means a commitment to printing a lot and keeping work in print – which was a policy, for example, of Centerprise in the early days, but is now proving financially impossible. Again we are returned to issues of organisation and support.

We shall have more to say about how the social relations that surround and sustain this work differ from those of the orthodox publishing world, and how much further we now want to go, in the light of what we have learned from the practices which now shape our aspirations. But we should also stand out of the way for a while and let you as readers take a substantial look at the work we are celebrating. These four passages – three extracts from autobiographies, one complete story – all come from the powerful and often traumatic experience of the entry into adult life through 'starting work'.

Ron Barnes: 'Licence to live'

I wanted to be a sign-writer. If I had had the right guidance, I would have wanted to be an artist, but to me sign-writing was an art. I got a reference from school which no employer even looked at and I found it very difficult to get a job as an apprentice, or even a learner.

'Well,' said Mum. 'You'd better go into the french polishing with Uncle Alf, then.'

My mother had always been a bit of a mystery to me. Here I was, an asthmatic child, being told by my mother to take up french polishing, among the fumes of polish, sawdust, and in very bad working conditions. All I could put this down to was that she didn't understand what sort of trade she was telling me to go into.

At last I managed to get a job from the labour, as a learner sign-writer in Stamford Hill. I rang the bell and waited. I then heard footsteps running down the stairs as though being chased. When the door came open I was then faced with the enormous body of Mr Davis. I never thought it possible for a man of his build to run downstairs like this.

'I'm enquiring about the job.'

'Oh yes, how old are you?'

'Fourteen, sir.'

'Don't call me sir, boy, for gawd's sake. No sir, er, Mr Davis'll do.'

'I have a reference here from my school. They think I would be suited to sign-writing.'

'Oh, never mind that, can you make tea?'

'Yes, sir – Mr Davis.'

'Are you strong?'

'Oh, yes s...'

'Do you think you could lift scaffold boards and push a barrow?'

'Oh yes, I could.'

I was hoping that my tone of voice would make me appear stronger than I looked.

'All right, kid, start Monday.'

Oh boy.

'Thank you sir Davis, er Mr Davis, thank you.'

I was full of joy that afternoon. Never again was I to experience the delight and sense of achievement that I got from getting my first job. I had visions of becoming a first class tradesman, with my own little box of paints and first class brushes and a palette. As soon as my parents came home I told them. Their reply was 'Oh good'. No questions, nothing. My mother wasn't on to me to start work to get some money from me, but it did hurt me deeply when little interest was shown at what I thought was a wonderful achievement. Maybe they were so depressed with their life of work and struggle and an unhappy marriage, that they could find no enthusiasm for anything. Or they may have been just plain indifferent. I don't know.

I reported for work on Monday morning at 8am. I made my way down the sloping alleyway, which was about five hundred yards long. I got to the bottom and there was the shed on the left. All around were scaffold boards, ladders and old shop facias. The two big doors to the shed were open. I looked inside to see two men, one about fifty and the other about twenty-five. The older man spotted me.

'Are you the new boy, then?'

'Yes, sir.'

'I'm Alf and him there is Ron. What's yours?'

'Er, my name's Ron as well.'

'Ah, be jassus, we can't have that now, can we? There's enough fucking confusion around here already. We'll call you Ronald. You ever used a brush, have you?' said Alf.

'Well, I have done a lot of drawing and painting and that.'

'Well forget all that, 'cause you won't be doing any drawing here. Do yer know the primary colours?' he asked.

'I do,' I replied.

'Have you ever mixed oil colours?'

'No, sir.'

'Alf, not sir!' he bawled. 'Well first of all you'd better make a cup of tea.'

This Irish foreman, Alf, was short but heavily built, with a mass of thick, curly black hair, a broad face, wide-set clear blue eyes, broad nose and a healthy red face. Although he only stood about five foot four, he was a fit and powerful man.

He showed me how to mix paints, and this was my job for a long time, before ever touching a sign-writing brush. After being there about five months I had still not been given the opportunity to use a writer. I thought, perhaps Alf doesn't think I could do it? At home I did a poster, and was inspired to write, 'God is Love'. It turned out beautiful. I thought that if I showed it to Alf he might have a better opinion of me. I couldn't have been more wrong.

'Oh, gawd, bloody blimey. Oh holy mother of God! What are you trying to do: convert me or something? Oh fucking hell, oh it's fucking good boy, fucking good to be sure!'

About a fortnight after this incident, I had a chance to try my hand on some ladders which had the firm's name on them and had to be gone over to liven them up a bit.

'Now then, Ron. I've got to go out on a job, find something for Ronald to do.'

Alf picked up his kit, made his way down the alley and disappeared.

'I know what you can do, Ronald,' said Ron. 'You can paint over the firm's name on them ladders.'

'What me?' I said.

'Yes. But you'll have to keep your eye open for him coming back. At least it's something for you to practise on, and anyway, there's nothing else for you to do.'

I mixed up my paints, got out the ladders, got a box to sit on, and away I went. After a while I could feel I was being watched. I slowly turned round and a few yards behind me was Ron.

'Good kid good. Look, Ronald, take no notice of him.'

'Oh Alf you mean.'

'Who else?' said Ron.

He came nearer so that he was right behind me.

'He's a funny bloke,' he said. 'Mind you he treated me rough when I first started, but what he did to you the other week was diabolical. But never mind kid you keep at it and you'll soon pick it up. It's easy enough writing when you've got the knack, but wait till you have to get up there on those bleeding scaffold boards with a force nine gale blowing up your arse, or when the sun plays on your back till you want to spew your ring up. And the bright colours don't help your eyes much; that's why old Alf's got a squint ain't it? Keep at it son.'

I had been writing for about an hour. Ron had just gone to put an order in for some colours at the office above our shed. Suddenly I felt someone behind me. It can't be Ron, I thought, he's in the office. Oh no, it can't be comrade Alf. I shouldn't have got so carried away with the job in hand. I slowly turned my head. As I did so, Alf's chin was almost resting on my left shoulder.

'Don't they look attractive enough for you' he said. 'And what makes you think your bleeding wobbly hand is going to improve them? What a liberty you've got. Wipe it off, Ron,' he bawled, 'come here!'

I was sweating hot and cold, and I felt I had committed a most terrible crime.

'Don't you dare let him do that fucking lark anymore, I'm telling you. In fact next time I've got a job outside you will come with me.'

What was going through his mind I was soon to find out during that same week.

'Righto! Ronald get that barrow!'

To me this barrow was a monster on iron treaded wheels of about three feet diameter.

'Now then get those four boards and four tressels and put them on the cart.'

The boards were about two inches thick, and about eight foot long. The tressels were about ten foot long. Ron could see how exhausted I was after the first three boards and made towards me.

'Leave him!' screamed Alf. 'He wants to be a sign writer so he's got to know how to handle ladders and push a barrow.'

Ron gave Alf a look of hatred, but said nothing, probably because if he did his life would be made a misery as well, or perhaps the sack, the most dreaded weapon of all. I finally lifted the last tressel onto the barrow.

'Now then' shouted Alf, 'put me coat on, that bucket and rags, and me kit. O.K. Ron we will see you tonight. I painted the shop front yesterday and I'm going to finish it today, I've got to write and varnish it. Right now then' he said, 'push like fuck!'

I look up the slope of the alleyway and thought god I'll never make that, the weight on the barrow must have been about seven hundredweight. Alf pushed it like wheeling a baby in a pram. As we got half way up the slope Alf eased off so that I had most of the weight.

'Come on' he shouted, 'don't leave it all to me'.

I couldn't even see over the barrow, if I was going straight or not, I was on the kerb side; the barrow must have moved out to the right when a bus just missed the front of the barrow as it passed. Alf jumped up like he was going into a complicated ballet step.

'Keep the fucking thing straight' he bawled. A woman must have heard this language as she passed, judging by the look of surprise on her face.

We eventually got to the job in Stoke Newington High Street. By this time I was sweating profusely, off came our coats and we began to put up our tressels. Alf got out his brushes and colours, made his way up the steps and settled down to write, leaving me at the bottom. I began to cool down and I began to feel cold.

'Alf! I'm breaking me neck' I called.

'Go in the shop, sod you, and ask if you can use theirs'.

I was to make this journey many times in the course of the day. Whether Alf's guardian angel spoke to him or not I don't know, but he shouted to me to come up to him. I had never been on a scaffold before, it must have been about twenty foot up, not very high, but for a novice it seemed about twice that height. I held on for dear life. As I got to the top of the tressels, and had to swing my leg over and onto the boards.

'Come on' cried Alf, 'don't shit your fucking self, just don't look down'.

I didn't want him to think I was scared so I stood as upright as I could, and made towards him. Then it happened: I had trodden on a part where two boards were over-lapping. I did a sort of tap dance where the performer leans the body forward and kicks back his legs alternately. There was Alf doubled over, holding his stomach, red in the face with glee, the happiest I had ever seen him, he was overcome with joy. His joy was quickly broken when on recovering himself he found his front covered in the red paint which was meant for the job. Where he had been leaning over, the small pots clipped to his pallet had tilted, the paint running down the front of his overalls.

'You clumsy git' he said, 'go down and get a cloth off the barrow. No, don't bother I'll go'.

After wiping himself down, he then gave me a brush and I was allowed to paint the inside of the letters, while Alf did the more skilled job of doing the outlines of the letters. After letting me do this my spirits began to rise, with visions of myself carrying my little box, with its paint and oils and brushes inside. I began to make my own sign-writing box, in my spare time in the yard, when I didn't have to mix paints or make boards for the shop fronts. But for some unknown reason Alf would harrass me at every occasion and try to dishearten me. At times I would go home through the back streets so as to hide my tears from passers-by. I was so unhappy with this man after me all the time, yet I was afraid to pack up in case I couldn't get another job in the sign-writing trade; heaven knows it was difficult enough getting this job let alone a second choice. I was unable to tell my parents my troubles, as they always seemed to be so distant, why I don't know, but there it was. So, when in bed I would pray. I had always prayed. God? I didn't even feel that I knew him or his son, there was no one else, so I prayed. Well, they told me in school to pray if I wanted something, so that's what I did. I got no answer. Alf kept after me, and I had to pack up, I could stand no more. Mr Davis could do nothing about it.

So much for job number one.

'I don't know why you don't go in for french polishing with your Uncle Alf,' my mother would say. After being out for about three months, I tried a little sign-writing shop in Stoke Newington Church Street. The owner didn't want to know if I could make tea, in fact he didn't want to know anything. 'Bring your cards on Monday' and that was it.

He was a big man with a big beard and of more gentle breeding than Alf. One mistake lost me this golden opportunity to learn the trade. Jackson had a small board to write in De Beauvoir Road. He gave me a large empty paint can, and a small one full of paint which was to paint the background with before writing. He also gave me some newspaper and said,

'Put the newspaper in the large can and then put the small tin of paint inside the big one.'

Due to my misunderstanding, I thought he wanted the small tin poured on to the newspaper that had been put in the large can, and this is what I did, thinking it was some kind of trade trick that I hadn't seen yet. When I had finished painting the board it looked shocking. Result: the sack.

Daisy Noakes: 'The town beehive— a young girl's lot'

A dormitory maid was wanted at Ovingdean School, so my sister Lily spoke for me.

This was November 1922, and I would be 14 in December, so an appointment was made for the interview.

Yesterday in blouse and gymslip, today unrecognisable in a costume my mother bought from a neighbour.

The coat reached my knees, the shirt my ankles. Around my shoulders a wide fox fur, its ugly head grasping the tail. On my head a large brimmed black hat, fitted with several foldings of newspaper inside to make it fit, and every wisp of hair out of sight.

We had a penny train ride to the Pier terminus, then proceeded to walk to Ovingdean by way of Sea Front, Kemp Town to the back of the East Brighton Golf Course, behind Roedean School, and down to Ovingdean. Although it was November, I was so hot with all the unfamiliar clothes I was wearing.

Mother told me to always add 'Ma'm' to every answer, and stand up when spoken to. By now I was getting a bit nervous, but knew I had to face it. We went round to the back door, as staff were never allowed to use the front door or the front drive.

The butler was called, and said 'I'll see if Madam will see you'. Yes, she would, so we were shown into the large drawing room. I was bewildered. I did not want to be in all this elaborate surroundings. Madam entered, and asked us to sit. I perched myself on one of the chairs, while Mum was asked if I was honest, hardworking, reliable, an early riser. (I did not know that would be 5.30am). To all this Mum replied that I was.

I was asked to stand up, and Madam said 'You will look taller when you have a longer skirt and hair done up in a bun'. She asked me how old I was. I replied '14 next month', so she said my wage would start at my age, £14 a year, with a 2/6d. a month rise at the end of a year, and I could start work as soon as I attained my 14th birthday.

Now began the preparation for my leaving home. I would need servant's uniform and a box to pack it in.

Mum and I went to the market where she bought a light coloured tin trunk. The lid was dented in, and between us we carried it home, taking a handle each. Dad got a plank of wood and a hammer, and banged the lid till the dent came out. Then Mum painted it with stove black paint all over and it stayed out in the yard several days, because of the strong smell the paint contained. When it seemed fit to bring indoors, Mum pasted wallpaper over the inside, and then it looked quite smart.

With materials wanted for my uniform I had to draw all my money from my Penny Bank. I had over £3 which seemed an enormous amount, but it was not enough for what I needed.

Mum made me two blue dresses for morning wear, half-lined, one black dress for afternoon wear, and four large bibbed white aprons. Fancy white aprons were not worn at the school till later. I had two Dorcas type caps for morning wear, frill caps for afternoons were supplied, one pair of ward shoes for mornings, one pair high-lows for afternoons and three pairs of black stockings, and lastly a pair of corsets. Oh, the agony, getting used to them after a liberty bodice, and quite unnecessary as I was so thin. My other underclothes would have to do. No new hat or coat, but I took my Sunday one, (and, as our time off duty was so small, there was no chance of wearing them out). Celluloid collar and cuffs.

My hours were from 5.30am to 10.30pm and no let-up anywhere during that time. How I stayed awake I do not know. My off-duty time was Tuesday 2.30pm to 9.30pm and one afternoon a fortnight for the same hours.

Mum helped me carry my trunk to the tram, and helped put it on the bus to Ovingdean. The bus then only stopped on the Coast Road, and my sister Lily should have been there to meet me.

The conductor helped me off with it and there I waited at the roadside, as one person cannot carry a tin trunk with any dignity. It was not long before Lily came into view and between us we reached the school and what was to be my bedroom, which I was to share with three other maids.

How bare it looked, a rail divided each section but the curtains were all pulled to the centre, four beds with one mattress on each, and a red blanket top cover, four washstands with jug in basin on top, mug and toothbrush dish underneath, and a chamber in each of the cubby holes at the bottom.

My sister was not one of my room-mates and I felt so miserable. At night I was afraid to completely undress. I put my nightie on top of my vest and knickers, and how I was going to use that chamber in the night if I needed it, I did not know.

I was nearest the light switch so it was my privilege to turn it off. I felt my way to my bed, and lay there thinking about running home, but I knew I would only be sent back, so cried at the thought when something went *bang* under my bed. It was my tin trunk reverting to its original shape, and from that moment my childhood ended, and I realised I had been launched on the world to earn my own living. 1923. I vowed no more tears but a 'stiff upper lip' was needed from now on.

Tomorrow started a new life in new surroundings and I'd prove I was somebody instead of one in a crowd.

Ernie Benson: 'To struggle is to live'

For me the New Year was to be my baptism as a worker. On the eve of my commencing work my father, who by now had 'jacked up' the peddling business and returned to work at the steelworks, said he would wake me before he left for work, which for him commenced at 6.00am. My starting time was 7.00am and finishing time 5.00pm.

And so it was that shortly before leaving he came upstairs, shaking me gently so as not to waken the others and whispering it was time to get up. It was a dark chill morning. Overnight there had been a fairly heavy fall of snow, which muffled the sound of the miners' and mill-workers' clogs. I trod quietly down the stairs and saw that father had lit a fire in the grate which was giving out warmth and light. He indicated the washing sink, saying 'Get thissen weshed fust afore breakfast,' and knowing this would be done, he put on his cap ready to go out, hesitated for a moment, then with a 'Look after thissen while tha's at wuk', he went out closing the door softly behind him. He had cut and wrapped up some sandwiches for me, there was steaming hot tea in the teapot, so I made my breakfast, but not before there was a slight creaking on the stairs and mother appeared, and started quietly bustling about, for my sister Caroline also had to go to work. It was going to take me a half an hour's walking to get to my place of work for Chas. Benn & Co. Boilermakers.

After my being rejected for a job on the *Yorkshire Evening Post* the juvenile employment office could only offer me work in the mines or engineering. Several of my cousins and a couple of uncles and many of the lads living around us worked down the mines, and having seen those who had been injured and heard various stories, I had decided I would work anywhere rather than underground. Some miners had to take journeys of nearly an hour to get to work by tram and shank's pony.

Thus it was that after I completed my breakfast, mother tied a scarf round my neck, buttoned my overcoat (things I could easily have done myself, but she seemed to want to do them), gave me a little hug and with an anxious 'Look after yourself love', stepped out of the door with me to see me off on my first working day.

I shall always remember that bleak morning, trudging along in the snow, head bent down trying to avert the cold wind and the flurry of snow flakes on my face. There were not many workers going in my direction and those who were seemed too numbed to bid a 'Good morning', with which most workers whether you knew them or not, would greet each other. Part of my journey was alongside the canal, whose black water contrasted sharply with the snow and there was the sight and sound of water lapping against the shadowy coal barges tied to the mooring posts on the canal bank. At last I entered the works, making my way to the timekeeper's office, on the outside walls of which hung the time clock. On the clock box a candle was burning and flickering in the draught from the door whenever it was opened. Apparently the firm had its own generator, but owing to the cold weather there had been some difficulty in starting the gas engine and until it started there could be no lighting.

Having punched my time card, I waited until someone should come along, and was looking round the dimly lit place wondering what I was going to do in it, when a gruff voice behind me said, 'You the new lad?' I nodded in answer to his question and the man said, 'Heng on a minute or two, the gaffer won't be long afore he's 'ere'.

At last the gaffer did appear and it was old Charlie Benn himself. For that day my duties were to be at the beck and call of the men in the works. The following day was pretty much the same, except that after carrying out most of the orders I was told to go and sweep the floor in the boiler house. One of the men took me there to show me what to do. It was nice and warm there. The boiler was a gas fired one and had a small oval iron cover in the front held in place with an iron bar propped against it because the latch to hold it in place was broken. I was told by the workman not to stand in front of the door because if the bar slipped the door would fall down and possibly shoot out flames. Sweeping up the floor even leisurely didn't take very long and nobody seemed to be worrying what I was doing. I sat on the barrow into which I had emptied the floor sweepings and began to enjoy the warmth of the place compared to the chilly atmosphere of the workshop and handling cold metal. The barrow was placed two or three feet away from the small oval cover. All of a sudden, the iron bar fell down with a clatter, the cover fell down and as it fell a long blue flame, I'll swear it was four feet long, shot out straight for my belly. I fell back into the barrow, then went yelling to tell one of the workmen what had happened. He came back with me, got another iron bar which he used to lift the cover in place, then replaced the bodger bar. Turning to me he grinned and said, 'Did it frighten you sonny?'

Just before 5.00pm the gaffer came to me and said he didn't want me to
go to the works the following day, but to go to another engineering works,
Joshua Buckton & Co., where I would join three of his men who were
engaged on a contract for steelwork on an extension to one of the
workshops there. Buckton's was still as far away to walk, but in the opposite
direction.

Next morning I reported there at 7.00am and asked where Charles
Benn's men were working. Someone took me along, for it was a huge place
to me and certainly, apart from the steelworks, I had never been in a factory
like it, with rows of benches and vices and machinery of various shapes and
sizes. My guide led me to where three men were stood around a brazier,
saying to them, 'I think this lad 'as to work wi' you', then left me with them.

The oldest man of the three, smoking a pipe and with arms folded, took
the pipe out of his mouth and with a stare that had the hint of a smile, said,
'New lad eh – what's your name?' I told him and then one of the younger
men looked a bit interested and said 'Tha wouldn't be Ginger Benson's lad
would tha?' I nodded at which the man went on, 'Ahr knaws 'im – wukked
wi' 'im once – if tha tuns aht as gooda wukker as 'im tha'll do'.

We stood around the brazier for a few minutes, then the old man who
was the leading hand and a Scot, knocked the dottle out of his pipe and said
briefly, 'Reckon we ought to start'. 'Jock' the man who said he knew
my dad, were rivetters, the other being the holder-up, the man who held the
rivetting 'dolly'. My job was to be rivet lad.

With a 'Come here', Jock took me to where the rivet fire was. It was an
iron pan on four steel legs with bellows underneath with a pipe which
connected with the pan. The pan itself was filled with coke which had a dull
red glow in the centre. Jock seized a handle at the side of the pan, moving it
rapidly to and fro and the full red glow sprang into life with sparks flying
upwards, turning from dull to bright red, then yellowy and then almost
white heat. 'Gimme some o' them rivets' he commanded, 'and now watch
what I do'. Placing the rivets in the fire he worked the bellows and as the
rivets changed colour and just appeared to be at sizzling heat he said 'Now
that's how we want 'em – no hotter or they'll burn, – see them little tongs?'
he indicated a small pair in a tray at the side of the pan, 'Give 'em to me an
I'll show you what to do.' With the tongs he picked out a rivet, then with a
'Coming over Sam', he tossed the rivet to his mate who caught it in a similar
pair of tongs before it hit the floor. It was all done neatly and expertly. 'Try
it' he said. After several attempts I began to get the knack of it and he
nodded approvingly, saying, 'That'll do, let's get started'.

I began to like the job and soon learned to get the rivets to the right heat
and toss them a bit more expertly. Those three men worked with a beautiful
rhythm. As soon as I tossed a rivet, one would catch it in tongs, the
holder-up would slam the dolly on the rivet head, then with hand flashing
for only seconds the rivetters hammered the rivets flat. They worked

amazingly quick and I had my work cut out to keep up the supply of rivets at the right degree of heat.

It was during a lull in the morning, when I had left some rivets in the firepan ready for a resumption of work, and had been away for a few minutes on an errand for the rivetters, that on my return I found a youth operating the bellows like one possessed. Shouting at him to stop it, I went up to him pointing out that he had burnt the rivets, but he answered quite impolitely and shoved me aside. At that I picked up the tongs and threatened to bash his face in if he didn't stop. He knew I meant it and though he was bigger he slunk away.

A few minutes later I saw a bowler hatted foreman speaking to the rivetters and pointing at me. Jock jerked his head for me to go over, and when I stood in front of them he said, 'Mr So-and-so here says that you were going to hit his son with a pair of tongs – is that right?' 'Yes' I said, 'and I'll tell you why', which I did and showed him the burnt rivets. Turning to the foreman (who had nothing to do with us) Jock said to him, 'Bugger off and the next time you come to us with a complaint, come with a straight story and you can tell that lad of yours that if I see him messing around here I'll kick him from arseholes to breakfast time'. As the foreman went away the other rivetter said, 'Tha did reight lad, ahr can see tha's a chip off the old block', and he rumpled my hair with his hand.

I worked with them for the rest of the week. When they were working on the overhead girders and doing cold rivetting, I would climb the stanchions with a couple of bags of rivets slung around my neck. Before I did this however, they asked me if heights worried me, but I didn't reckon fifteen or twenty feet was high – not after climbing pylons of thirty feet and more and sitting on the cross members at the top for a 'dare' when I was still at school.

I drew my wages for a fifty hour week on the Saturday morning, receiving my first wage packet of 10/d. On the Monday morning I had to return to our workshop and after the usual morning errands and tea brewing, the gaffer thought up a new job for me – picking up rivets lying around the shop floor, sorting them out, then placing them in appropriate boxes. Almost in the centre of the workshop was a big machine, the base of which was below the shop floor. The main drive belt itself was below the floorboards, which could be lifted out and removed in the event of the belt breaking, when it would be much easier to repair. Some rivets had fallen below through gaps in the floorboards, but as the machine was running I left them there. Later on the gaffer came round and it was obvious he had been checking on my work; calling me over to where the big machine was, he lifted up one of the boards and said, I hadn't done my work properly. 'Look at all those rivets', he said. My reply was that the machine was running and I was afraid of the big belt. He said it was nonsense and there was nothing to be afraid of, but seeing that I was afraid he said, 'Pick 'em up when it stops'. Clearly he wasn't pleased with my attitude, so just after lunch he told me he had another job for me in the basement stores. This was a fairsized place, dark and cold, lit by a single forty or sixty watt bulb.

Under this light, on the floor, stood a big many-spoked pulley about four feet in diameter. This was the job – he wanted me to clean all the rust from the spokes and hub ready for painting. Actually a scaling hammer was required, but instead he handed me an old 14" half round file, and, after showing how it could be used for chipping and scraping the rust off, left me to it. What a miserable hole it was with that single lamp and no heating and in the first week or so of January.

However I set to, in an effort to keep warm more than anything else. Pausing after a vigorous effort, I thought I heard a very faint slithering sound and looked rather nervously towards the more shadowy sides of the basement, but couldn't see anything. Several times I thought I heard this almost inaudible noise, then I saw a dark shape gliding across the floor, where the fringe of light from the light bulb merged with the shadows. There was no mistaking, it was a rat and not alone either for in its wake there was another. Now I never liked rats – neither the four-legged or two-legged and I'll confess I was afraid, remembering a story about a man who worked in the Paper Mill, who was trying to kill a rat he had cornered, when it sprang and bit him in the throat, causing an infection from which he later died.

A little before 5.00pm the gaffer came to see how I had progressed and expressed his displeasure at what he considered a small amount, and said I would have to work on it the following day. 'No I won't' I said, 'Yer can stick the job up your arse, I'm not working with rats about.' My outburst astonished him and he said, 'I don't think you'll be much good to me' and feeling saucy I told him I thought his workshop was not going to be much good to me either.

That night I walked home wondering what I was going to tell my parents about chucking up my job. Nevertheless I told them all about it, omitting any mention of the swear word I'd used. Father was a bit amused, asked how much I'd been paid for the weeks work I'd put in, then said I must go back the following day and demand payment for the day I had worked and also to ask for an extra 4/-, being a 1/- a day out-working allowance for the previous week when I worked at Buckton's and to tell the gaffer that he (dad) had told me to ask for it. 'Also' he added, 'if he wants to know who your dad is, say Ginger Benson and if he doesn't give it to you, I'll be walking down to collect it myself'.

Next day I went to the works and old Charlie Benn asked what I was doing there; he started to crib about the 4/- saying I wasn't worth it and who had told me? But when I said Ginger Benson was my father he thrust the money in my hand shouting, 'Get out of the bloody shop' and I was happy to get it. Father laughed when I told him about it and said, 'He knows what I know abaht him and he'd been a bit frightened if I'd gone dahn'.

Janice Day: 'A break with routine'

'It's just a little something to remind you of us all'. Hilary placed the package on the post desk.

'Thanks very much, I didn't expect anything'. My embarrassment showed on receiving my first leaving present.

I opened the wrappings which revealed a small carved elephant.

'They never forget', explained Dave, 'We thought it would make a good present. We won't forget you in a hurry'.

I smiled at Dave. He'd been trying to get a date with me since my first day at the bank. Six months and three days later he was no longer hopeful.

'Perhaps', I thought, 'his best friend should tell him'.

Still he had been kind and more than helpful to me in my first job. I'd replaced him as junior, he had now reached the exulted position as junior counter clerk. He'd explained my duties to me:

8.30 arrive, sign in (the junior's name was always first in the book). Sort out post. Open head office sack. Distribute accordingly. Make coffee as soon as Mr. Williams (Bank manager) arrives. Mr. Williams and Mr. Rice (Sub manager) have cups and saucers, everyone else mugs. After collecting and washing dirty cups report to machine room for sorting of cheques and recording control (debits and credits taken over the counter) punching of statements, transmission of previous day's work to Head Office. After lunch do post until 3.00 then make tea. When washing up finished, return to machine room to finish recording control; then finish post. Take post to post office on way home.

'I'll never cope' I thought that morning, but after a few weeks I had the routine off pat. That was when the trouble started.

My first blunder had been one made by most juniors. Breaking the clip in the head office sack. The sack was a canvas bag, into which internal memos etc were zipped and then the zip sealed with a clip. I managed to break the clip while the zip was still fastened. Dave came to the rescue. His boy scouts penknife, the bit for getting stones out of horses hooves, soon solved the problem.

'There you go' he beamed, 'Now let's get the post out before you do anything else'.

'Thanks Dave', my relief was short lived as I gazed at the memos appearing from the sack.

'But that's what I sent off last night to head office'.

'Oh! Jan, you forgot to turn the address label round', Dave seemed to think it all a great joke, and wasted no time in relating the story to the others.

'Well', remarked Bob, assistant machine officer, 'You're a fully-fledged junior now; we all did that during our term of office'.

'Don't worry', said Hilary, now a fully-fledged counter clerk. 'Send the head office sack off this morning, no-one will say anything'.

'I suppose so' I sighed, 'But I must remember to change the address this time.

I had just lived down this episode when fate struck again. There were no washing facilities on the ground floor of the bank so twice a day I had to carry the dirty cups up a narrow flight of stairs to the ladies. The banking hall was always busy around tea-time, and I collected the dirty cups as discreetly as possible. There was the kind of hush you get in libraries as I carried the tray of crockery up the stairs. I'd reached the last but one stair when my foot slipped and down fell Janice, tea-cups and all. In the echo chamber of the stair well it sounded like the 1812 overture. The sound reached into the manager's office, and even brought Rosemary and Derek up from the basement, where each afternoon they spent half an hour 'getting things straight'. I was soon surrounded by anxious faces.

'You ok… quick Dave bring a blanket' Bob, the bank's first aid certificate holder, took control 'Now just stay still while I see if anything's broken'.

'I'm f.f.f.fine' I stammered, tears streaming.

'Janice, what a noise' Rosemary looked more flustered than me.

'Keep still everyone, I've sounded the alarm!' Norman the messenger appeared waving his truncheon.

My laughter was forced from me.

'It's shock', stated Bob. 'She's having hysterics'.

The customers were leaning over the counter, trying to get a sighting of the bank robbers. Fortunately Mr. Rice managed to forestall the police, so the incident was kept 'within the family'.

The shock waves from my next escapade reached the whole of the Westminster network. On the last Friday of each month all branches had to punch out a Form 28. This was a summary of the branch's work during the previous month. The tape was transmitted to H/O and fed into the computer memory banks to tie in with all the other Form 28s. This particular Friday our branch was short-staffed. Rosemary, who, as Senior Machine Officer, usually processed the form, was absent with her monthly migraine. Bob and Derek seconded to the Chigwell branch. The rest of the staff were dealing with the customers. Which left me in charge of the Form 28. Being well aware of the need for accuracy I took my time preparing the tape. In fact I took so long that there was only just time to transmit it to H/O.

Mr. Rice was really very kind on the Monday morning, all things considered that is. It seemed I had omitted to punch out the X on the form, mainly because I didn't know I had to, thus throwing the monthly figures for Westminster Bank into disorder.

'Of course, under normal circumstances this responsible task would never have been given to a junior, Mr. Rice peered over his reading glasses. 'I'm very sorry, it won't happen again'. What more could I say.

'For the time being, any tapes prepared by you, will be checked, until you have become more accustomed to machine work' his voice was suitably stern.

I gave my notice in the following Friday, and now I was in Mr. Rice's office saying my farewells.

'We'll be sorry to see you leave, you certainly livened the branch up', Mr. Rice's relief was evident, 'Don't forget us'.

'I won't Mr. Rice, and thankyou', I shook his hand and left banking to enter the world of journalism. My next job was on the local paper, of course I was starting as junior. Making the tea and doing the post, but who knew where that might lead.

Collision course with literature?

So far we have talked about some of the reasons why people start to write − pressure to communicate, if you like − and we have begun to sketch some of the forms of communication which people may find themselves part of, as this writing is circulated locally and from group to group. But this is already a historical jump; it supposes as the social reception of writing the pull from the outside, something which has only existed recently and which exists imperfectly even now. It leaves out what was there before, to make it worth the labour of creating names and forms and finding hearers for what would otherwise stay in silence. What was there before was shaped by a particular set of myths about writing and breaking into print.

Writing does have a very particular magic to it. The idea that you can, with very little equipment, set down something which only you have made, and which can give meaning to who you are and what has happened to you; and the idea that this can be reproduced in thousands of copies and come back to you in a form which can help you recognise yourself in a new way, be recognised by others as you wish to be recognised, *and* enable you to live without the normal constraints of waged work, i.e. make *money*... all that is, it must be admitted, a bit magic! With my pen, the fantasy goes, I can at a stroke alter my entire relationship to the culture, and move from the galleys to the bridge of my own ship. And I can do it, seemingly, all by myself, with the aid, at most, of a few kind gentlemen from offices in Bloomsbury with access to the magic market. None of all that nonsense about cleaning other players' boots for five years. Anyone can do it, and, as the advertisements put it, in only ninety days! It's so magic that many of us keep it in reserve in a drawer, a resort so potentially important that it is better never finally to try because it would be so awful to fail.

It would be silly to deny the power of all this — and silly for us, in the Federation, to deny its relation to the realities as well as the myths of the contemporary publishing industry. We have learned from many experiences just how attractive this magic is — to ambitious individuals or, to put it more kindly, to people who want to make a bob or two. Individual groups in the Federation have been put under considerable strain through the individual 'success' of some members outside the Federation, for example on television or in the theatre.

And yet we know, too, that the publishing industry isn't structured around the nurturing of new and unpractised writers, and isn't at bottom interested in our struggles with our forms of truth. The experience of working in community bookshops has given us a clear idea how bookselling is now about the intensive promotion of a few dominant genres (of fiction and non-fiction) which push everything else into the margins. What follows is a sketch rather than a portrait, but we have to leave it to those more intimate with the industry to elaborate it.

The politics of publishing

Most publishers have now been taken over by major multi-nationals or conglomerates. They are now run like any other capitalist industry, with the finance and marketing departments well to the front of decision-making and editorial departments well in the rear.

The fiction industry seems set to self-destruct... The current crisis is rooted in the deeper problem triggered by the American inspired paperback revolution of the early 1970's. Then a traditionalist industry was transformed by mass marketing. Novels were promoted on TV and radio, writers sent on nationwide tours, and dump bins began to appear in supermarkets and bookshops... Now the industry is placing increasing reliance on a *single* novel each year, preferably by one of the brand names: Higgins, Ludlum, Le Carré, Maclean, King, Straub. —*Time Out*, December 1980.

Best-selling books Sunday Times, 20.9.81

Figures in brackets give last week's positions. Final figures indicate number of appearances in listings.

General

1 (3) *Rothman's Football Yearbook 1981-82* Jack Rollin (Queen Anne's Press £5.95/7.95)1

2 (1) *Invitation To a Royal Wedding* Kathryn Spink (CLI £7.95) 5

3 (4) *Me and My Camera* Joe Partridge (Ash and Grant £4.95) 1

4 (5) *Guinness Book of British Hit Singles* Tim and Joe Rice, Paul Gambaccini and Mike Read (Guinness £4.99) 7

5 (9) *Cosmos* Carl Sagan (Macdonald £12.50) 16

6 (7) *The Lord God Made Them All* James Herriot (Michael Joseph £6.95) 13

7 (—) *In The Fast Lane* Geoffrey Boycott (A. Barker £6.95) 3

8 (8) *James Herriot's Yorkshire* Photos by Derry Brabbs (Michael Joseph £8.50) 92

9 (6) *The Royal Wedding* Brenda Ralph Lewis (Purnell £2.50) 5

10 (—) *Second Book of Bricks* Robert Morley (Weidenfeld £4.95) 0

Fiction

1 (3) *Voices in the Garden* Dirk Bogarde (Chatto £6.50) 1

2 (—) *River of Death* Alister Maclean (Collins £6.95) 0

3 (1) *Noble House* James Clavell (Hodder £8.95) 13

4 (—) *July's People* Nadine Gordimer (Cape £5.95) 0

5 (2) *Luciano's Luck* Jack Higgins (Collins £6.95) 5

Paperbacks

1 (—) *Unreliable Memoirs* Clive James (Picador £1.50) 0

2 (2) *Mastering Rubik's Cube* Don Taylor (Penguin 95p) 9

3 (1) *The Prince and Princess of Wales' Wedding Day* (Pitkin £1.95) 3

4 (3) *Not 1982* (Faber £2.99) 5

5 (10) *The Flame Trees of Thika* Elspeth Huxley (Penguin £1.50) 1

6 (6) *The Prince and Princess of Wales* (Jarrold £1.00) 5

7 (—) *The Simple Solution to Rubik's Cube* James J Nourse (Bantam 95p) 6

8 (8) *The Girl in a Swing* Richard Adams (Penguin £1.50) 8

9 (—) *Dr Fischer of Geneva or The Bomb Party* Graham Greene (Penguin £1.25) 0

10 (5) *Firestarter* Stephen King (Futura £1.95) 1

Agents like Carol Smith are already *commissioning* fiction – literally sending out plots to suitably hungry tyros… Carol Smith is not in the business of promoting writers, or even selling novels, but of setting up deals. She prides herself on disabusing her clients of their literary pretensions and re-directing them towards what will sell. —'Into the dump bin', *Time Out*, December 1980.

Books are published with a shelf-life like tuna fish or condensed milk of six months, after which they will be pulped. Some will be top of the best-selling list before they are published, like the old Beatles records used to be.

Fewer and fewer first novels are published every year, and those normally in hardback editions of 1-2,000, distributed almost exclusively through libraries. (Federation books usually work on first-print runs of 1-2,000 and don't wait for the author to win the Booker Prize before they re-print.) The number of publishers who publish new poetry is very small, and most collections are by poets who have established a reputation through the important magazines. Group collections of poetry, of the kind Federation groups have favoured, rarely appear. The small presses and little magazines, though sharing with us many arguments about the way subsidy runs on main lines in predictable directions, tend to be coteries rather than open associations, marginal forms rather than oppositional ones. (A sign of what we mean by lack of openness is the frequent absence of even a contact address – on a book of poems.)

There is more to say, some of which will be said later, about the connections between the prestige end of publishing and the literary establishments of universities and the Arts Council. The point to make here is that these are all forms of organisation of literature, and that they stand in the way of new forms that develop for new needs, and that for all but a few messages, they act as silencers rather than megaphones. We are not complaining simply that they fail to recognise the interest and the potential of working-class social history, local studies, poems and stories. On the contrary, since the market was opened up by the history workshop movement and local publishing initiatives, parallel books have appeared on many lists. OUP has a series of 19th century reminiscences which includes *A London Child in the 1880's*, *Hooligan Nights* and *The Diary of a Victorian Poacher*, and among the more popular imprints, Coronet has *Binder, Twine and Rabbit Stew*, Pan has *Mother Knew Best* and *Reuben's Corner*, and Penguin *The Book of Boswell*. Good books, all of them. Much more valuable than *Confessions of a Travel Courier* or *I was Hitler's Chiropodist*. But even as they move towards contemporary writers in this vein – including, as is already happening, some writers who started in Federation groups – they will not be able to do more than lift out end-products from a process they have had nothing to do with.

Co-operative forms

It has taken labour and thought to move away from the forms of work of the publishing industry – one of whose characteristics is the division of labour to the point where responsibility for the shaping of the whole work gets removed from the writer, dispersed and lost. In the beginning, except in their local scale of operation, some of the publishing groups in the Federation worked in much the same way as conventional publishers as far as the author could see. A manuscript would be sent or brought in, was mysteriously judged by unknown readers, just as mysteriously designed, typeset, produced and distributed. This was certainly the case with Centerprise, Stepney Books and People's Press of Milton Keynes. But it soon became clear that while you might have a different product, it was hard for the writer (let alone a reader) to be clear in what ways it was different. Writers could be left feeling that though they were not paid, money was being made by someone somewhere.

But as the movement developed we learned how to work *with* writers at every stage of making the book. Either in dialogue or in a wider group or in team work, interventions were made, passages were re-written, re-taped, bits deleted, additions asked for... then the making of the pages themselves, the choice of type, the placing of the pictures, the search for new pictures beyond the writer's own family album, the lettering at the start of each part or chapter, the design of the cover, the price, what else should be said in the book other than the author's main text (about the group and the Feder-ation by way of introduction, or invitation for further submis-sions)... all this began to be done collectively. Certainly technolo-gies played a part here – undoubtedly it is easier to do all this when working with offset litho, which makes it easier for everyone con-cerned to shape the final page exactly as it will be issued.

In this way, the writer and the workers learned more about the making of books and once this is learned it's hard to look at any printed matter as if it had just arrived on the page without a complex labour process. Many groups try to share this knowledge more widely, through workshop sessions or through exhibitions that show the growth of a book through re-drafting on paper, or through the stages of editing and commentary on a transcript of a tape. A look at a typed draft often shows objections or suggestions by the typist – another invisible worker made visible; then typesetting, negatives, plates, unbound sheets and the finished product are shown. Teach-ing the processes towards print has become a feature of much adult literacy work too, to try to break down the distant, authoritative and often threatening nature of the disembodied final tract.

Celebrating and sharing writing

Launching a book made in this way is an important social celebra-tion. Rather than being an exercise in publicity management, a launching is an occasion for bringing all the people who helped create the book together: writers, lay-out people, typists, printers, other writers in the project, friends, families, neighbours and so on. The reading of part of the text is, of course, the highlight. There have been launchings in pubs, community centres, cafes, railway station buffet rooms, trade union buildings, cinemas, where large numbers of people have gathered to listen to an evening of readings of autobiography, poetry, new writings by literacy students read by themselves to large audiences. This kind of display of the self-confidence generated by the new social relationships of writing and reading, are, for the majority of those attending, very important moments in the dis-establishing of literature and the mystique of publishing. For every reading is always permeated by the assumption that listeners are now potential writers themselves. *Under Oars*, a lighterman's autobiography published by Stepney Books and Centerprise jointly, was launched in a Thames-side pub and attended by dozens of retired and still working lightermen, trade union officials, families and friends, many of whom hadn't seen each other for twenty or thirty years. Parts of the book were read by the author's son to a packed pub listening in complete quiet. *The Island* was launched in a school built on the site of the old Island neighbourhood, with an exhibition of old photographs and amplified tape-recordings. It brought together people, who had been dispersed through re-development from as far away as Kent and Essex, in a re-creation of the neighbourhood which had finally disappeared 15 years earlier. *Every Birth it Comes Different* was launched in the Centerprise coffee bar, packed by Hackney Reading Centre students, their families and friends, and visitors from other centres, and the evening was an extraordinary blend of private and public; women read aloud written accounts of the birth of their children to eighty or more people.

Launching parties are part of selling the books, as are all public readings. It's quite a different thing to buy a book which has just spoken to you in the person of its writer. When the East Bowling History Workshop in Bradford launched its first publication, *Bowling Tidings,* in a local social club, 400 copies from a first print run of 1000 were sold in half an hour. Many groups, particularly writers' workshops, have made it a priority to read in public, at schools, colleges, local festivals, political events and pub evenings, and simply on exchange visits to each other. Apart from the inevitable bookstall and the sales it achieves, this *is* distribution of literature, and creates a wider audience than book production alone can do. In some groups the balance tilts strongly this way, with reading dominanting over publishing; some have developed towards performance of songs, sketches and drama, like the Controlled Attack group which has strong links with writers' groups in Tower Hamlets.

Questions of reading and distribution

Different work, reflecting popular experience; different writers, whom you may know and can certainly meet; different distribution, through local centres and face-to-face contacts – all these have created new reading publics. Examples tell the story best. Poetry is supposed to be a minority interest and yet the collection of poems by Vivian Usherwood sold over 10,000 copies, of which it is likely that nearly half were sold from one bookshop, Centerprise in Hackney. They were bought in dozens by friends of his, by relations, by other black teenagers and parents, by school teachers who used them in the classroom and by people who were prepared to try out such an attractive small collection at such a cheap price. the first edition was sold for 5p. It had a printed cover, was duplicated inside, folded and stapled by hand. Today, printed and stapled (or 'finished') commercially, this collection continues to sell at a still low price of 30p.

New readership can become new writers. A young woman, Christine Gillies, read Vivian's poems and decided to bring her own very personal poems to Centreprise for consideration. One of those poems was directly inspired by one of Vivian's and was a kind of reply to it. Half of the first edition of Jack Davitt's collection of poems, *Shipyard Muddling,* was sold in Swan & Hunter's shipyard where he worked on Tyneside. An ex-miner from Crumlington, Northumberland went around the numerous social clubs in his area, asking the club secretaries to announce on the tannoy that he was in the bar with his new book for sale. In five weeks he had sold 600 copies out of a print run of 1,500. Another example – in 1974 a retired carpenter, Albert Paul, took a manuscript of his early autobiography to the Brighton community newspaper, *QueenSpark.* They decided to publish it and the book was typed, designed, pasted up, cut and stapled by local voluntary labour. The pages were printed by a small local press. 2,000 copies were sold within three months, the majority in one small neighbourhood. It was sold door to door mostly, and Mr Paul himself sold 700 to friends and in cafes and streets.

QueenSpark have set a lot of store by this method of selling as a logical extension of the aim to make all the processes of producing and distributing visible, to challenge the concessions to commercial structure that are involved when selling through bookshops. One important gain is keeping the price low, thereby terminating the need to add the distributor's percentage. It can be done as collectively as any of the earlier processes. It encourages people to see writing and publishing as a neighbourhood activity growing out of, and nourishing, other social actions and contacts. It allows conversations to develop which give the writer feedback from readers, or may lead to writing being pulled out of a bottom drawer, or photos being offered for a street newspaper, or memories – too short for a book but long enough for an article – being told. It's one highly successful form for some groups of the *work* that must go on to stop the product of all these diverse activities being absorbed as just a commodity for sale on a shelf. Where this cannot be done, other ways have to be found of keeping the space open around the book.

Where groups haven't the social organisation, or the close neighbourhood in which to work like this, they have to rely more on shops for distribution and sales, and this takes us into a field of unresolved problems. They are less acute when the shops are the community bookshops, with which local publishing has developed in close association. Indeed it is the experience of working in these shops and selling our books through them that has boosted our confidence enough to say that the crude averages of bestseller lists do not represent any live 'popular taste'. These shops may include many books apart from our own, on topics from pruning roses to natural childbirth or a new children's picture book but the stock certainly includes books which have been made close to the readers' own lives. The problem comes when we (as we surely must) try to sell outside our own neighbourhoods, or insert our books among those in the mass distribution outlets. The main problem is price – the distributor takes roughly 50% of the cover price. In turn the bookshop usually takes 33%. Even when we hold down production costs, these can push the price of a book out of the reach of its local market. One solution has been adopted by Centreprise after years of deliberation: a two tier price system. Centreprise's more recent books have a Hackney price and a higher price for elsewhere. This is only a provisional answer and it may be that distribution is the next aspect the Federation will need to learn to organise and control.

When we say we are on a collision course with literature as it is conceived and established, we don't mean that all our activities are designed to confront, challenge or harass it. We merely suggest that if the kind of literary production *we* are engaged in were to become the norm – i.e. co-operative, associative, aiming at two-way (many way) communication, cheap, widely available, producing much in order to find out what our 'bests' are – then the conventional norm – competitive, elitist, profit-controlled, labour-dividing, separating producer from consumer – would be impossible (and in the meantime, the prevalence of the existing norm makes the establishment of ours uphill work in spite of its satisfactions). The techniques of mass community production are particularly painful when we encounter them in the world of cultural production, because it is there that we try to locate our expectations about breaking our silences, about sharing meanings and ideas. For all the work that has been done towards dis-establishing *this* literature, the creation of more reciprocal relations between readers and writers, this is still only a beginning.

Producing contradictions

Four years ago, Ken Worpole, in an afterward to the FWWCP's anthology *Writing*, put the problem this way:

Let us here honestly admit a problem. On the one hand, shoe-string publishing opens up possibilities for working class creation and communication outside the commercial and state-controlled media. On the other hand, the more important and widespread this alternative publishing becomes, the bigger the economic threat it may seem to pose to people working in the printing trade.

We can best try to take up the problem from this point.

This section was nearly not included. The problems talked about in this book were discussed frequently by the various contributors but this particular chapter, which we had rather grandly entitled 'Contradictions in the Labour Process in Local Publishing' seldom entered our conversation.

It wasn't that people didn't see it as a problem, they certainly did. But it was evidently such a hot potato that no-one wanted to take it up. The difficulty is implicit in our day to day operations, the way in which we actually conduct our work, 'make' our books, relate to other organisations and regulate our internal affairs. It obviously wasn't something we could duck, even had we really wanted to, though when it first came up – at the fag end of another discussion on some much more grandiose problem like 'culture' – our various reactions made it evident that here, at least, we did not think alike.

Who's digging whose grave?

None of us would wish to compete with, act against or actively undermine another form of working-class association or expression, and whatever else they may be trades unions certainly come within that category. Or, at least, we wouldn't want to *say* that that's the game we're in.

It's immensely uncomfortable to think that digging where you stand may amount to digging someone else's grave. So the first thing we want to register here is how close we came to *not* confronting the problems of our own practices. We also feel obliged to record two of the comments made at the meetings when the issue finally did come up.

The first of these was, 'Oh well, really anyone can learn it in twenty-four hours.' The second: 'We're only making work they wouldn't have anyway.'

We want to register these responses because the first demonstrates the power — our *power* — to determine the conditions upon which Labour will be hired is a power *they* resent most intensely, the second because it's the argument of the industrial revolution. We want to note this because it reflects both our own 'touchiness' about the whole convoluted issue and, perhaps more importantly, because it also reflects a very deep-seated ambivalence, not to say occasional antipathy, towards the trade unions and unease about positive expression of their (limited) power. This ambivalence is not something we will lightly escape from.

Why that should be is, on reflection, fairly obvious. Most of this book is devoted to our external relationships, to the way we relate (or don't relate) to the world outside our groups; this section, amongst other things, is about the way we relate to the world inside these groups. One thing that emerged from our discussions was that we were very sensitive about the manner in which *we* produced our various goods (i.e. the labour process involved). It was easy enough to agree that capitalism had an inbuilt propensity to divide the labour process (i.e. the making of things be they soap powders or computers) into smaller and smaller sub-units (in earlier days no less than 39 separate operations were involved in the making of a pin). And this process (increasingly dependent on 'impersonal machinery') removes people further and further from any direct relationship with the finished product (they find themselves making car door handles as opposed to cars). It also takes away the 'skill' necessary to make things, and to possess a skill ensures a good bargaining position (hence the working class tradition of learning a trade).

All of this was obvious. But precisely what were the characteristics of our own labour process? And what were the relationships between our labour process and trades unions? If capitalistic production was always going to be marked by such a division of labour was the same to be true of oppositional production? There were no easy answers.

As capital constantly divided the labour process, labour responded by craft trade unionism and later resistance through demarcation disputes and restrictive practices. Trade unionism itself emerged as a response to this capitalist sub-division of labour, and is largely a form of organised resistance for better conditions and material standards of living, using weapons defined by capitalism. The major weapon in such a conflict is the withdrawal of labour from the process of production; that is dis-connection, rather than the demand to produce in different ways or to produce different things. Here one could point to the apparent acquiescence of trades unions in the sacking of Mike Cooley, one of the leading figures in the Lucas aerospace alternative production project (which tried to show how the workers there, rather than being made redundant, could be employed producing such eminently useful goods as kidney machines). Despite such recent manifestations of interest in alternative ways of producing things as the Wales TUC visit to Mondragon in the Basque country (with its complex of interlocking co-operative establishments, the most successful in Europe), alternative ideas are still largely of last resort status. (Though that last resort is becoming increasingly frequent, as with the TGWU's decision to form a shirt-making co-operative from the bankrupt wreckage of a private firm). There is also an entrenched revolutionary Leninist opposition to such alternative ventures as in this SWP article:

We in the Socialist Workers Party have always argued in the past and will continue to argue in the future that all alternatives are diversionary. They are not the answer to the bosses' present vicious attacks on our organisation and our living standards. —*19th September 1981, article on co-operatives.*

Workers as employers

Many of our own groups, including the actual Federation, have found themselves at various times in the far from easy position of employers of labour. Being employers (often of people who are themselves members of/active in the various groups) has involved us in certain processes which can conflict with the interests of those employed. To put it at its simplest, some (though not all) of our interests as groups lie in getting things done as cheaply as possible. Lie there not because we want to make a 'profit' but because, firstly, we don't have enormous capital resources and, secondly, because cheapness means a wider distribution of a greater number of books. Certainly no-one's going to make a fortune working for any of our groups, but when paid labour is employed there is an immediate division between it and unpaid labour. Arguments in favour of the former are obvious. So much work needs to be done, a lot of it in the daytime, organising, visiting, setting up working groups, that here is an opportunity to create paid employment for one or more persons. But at once tensions develop. Contracts of employment have to be drawn up specifying hours, wages and conditions. But there is often an implicit assumption that what is written down as conditions of employment is a minimum expectation, the reverse of what one would expect in other jobs. Why are people who work in alternative projects expected to work longer and for less money? Largely because their employers are friends and fellow activists who put their commitments into such projects voluntarily.

But it's more than that. It's also because there is a deep distrust within the movement of anything which looks like the professional-isation of politics or cultural development – the creation of 'experts' with a vested interest in running affairs, with a propensity (to put it no stronger) to take decision-making out of the hands of the membership. Another fear is that paid workers will become the 'representatives' of projects or movements, the ones whose views are most often heard because they are most readily available to attend meetings or be interviewed by local radio. This has the effect of disenfranchising the group from coming to collective opinions. These are real fears because it has been the experience of many groups that outside agencies cause full-time workers to see them-selves as representatives rather than the employees that they actually are. Radio stations ring up, 'We're doing this programme tomorrow on the breakdown of community life, can you come and give us an angle on this?' Or someone from the Town Hall rings up to say that there's a meeting on Friday to talk about another weekend festival, and can the paid worker come to suggest what role local writing can play in it. The fact is that the cycle of democracy for most self-organised voluntary organisations is monthly whereas the cycle of capitalist and local government is daily. It is always tomorrow that they need someone to come to a meeting. The more the paid worker responds to such pressure the more disenfranchised and de-activated the voluntary group becomes.

One solution here is obvious – don't employ paid labour. Indeed many of our groups have a strong aversion to taking on full-time workers, and many others seek to limit the time any one person can be employed. In Manchester Commonword, people are only able to work for pay for three years. The first three paid workers who started Centreprise all agreed beforehand to the term of three years. The Federation itself appoints on a yearly basis, though such appointments can be re-negotiated for another year. But these are solutions which carry their own inbuilt problems. We would not be over-fond of jobs in other spheres with an inbuilt redundancy guillotine. Even without that problem, short term contracts paying people for a forty hour week, but expecting them to put in sixty, cause groups to employ particular kinds of people (the young, the unattached, mobile, those with no great financial or personal commitments). Refusing to engage any kind of paid labour can move groups to have most of their work done by the aged, the unwaged and those in jobs with flexible hours (like night education). Where there are no easy answers, each solution carries with it its own problems as groups experiment with various ideas such as job-sharing, attaching the payment to the work and so on.

Technologies and their contradictions

Nor is this the only problem we face, for it is not just a question of relationships with paid labour inside our groups; it is also a problem of the avoidance of paid labour, or the undercutting of paid labour, outside them. When the community press started in the late 1960's it did so very much on the basis of 'we must control the means of production ourselves'. The new offset litho technology has made it possible for many people to learn basic printing and plate-making on small A4 and A3 machines. Similarly, access to an electric typewriter with a carbon ribbon makes elementary typesetting easy. Also it was very much part of the ideology then that campaigning groups, ethnic groups, tenants' associations and so on should do the whole typing, layout and design and printing process themselves for their leaflects and street newspapers. A number of early community press projects bought machines for which they lacked sufficient work, with the result that they often went out looking for commercial work and, in the process, sometimes undercut unionised firms and unionised labour.

Nonetheless the problem of the relationship between our groups and union shops is one of considerable importance for a number of reasons. On the one hand, since one of our key aims is to liberate a whole production process (i.e. the making of books) for popular, unconditional access, we are in a sense directly or indirectly impinging upon those who make their living out of just that process. In a certain sense, since we are saying 'anyone can do it' we are taking the 'trades' out of 'trades unionism'. At the same time, part of our ability to operate in the way in which we do depends upon the availability of certain technologies. But technology isn't neutral. Just as we are trying to utilise its potential, so are capitalist firms – witness the way in which some academic publishers are now asking for camera-ready copy (i.e. for the author to do what amounts to the typesetting) as are many newspapers and magazines, particularly for display advertisements. In many ways the *scale* (as well as the motive) is very different, we aren't employing £50,000 computer based printing systems or £5,000 word processors; to us 'new technology' often means a typewriter and a tape-recorder.

But in some senses the problem is the same: it's about the ability, the right of organised (i.e. unionised) labour to dictate the terms (or bargain about them) upon which changes in production processes are made. That arises with our groups in two ways. Firstly a sensitive moment in production is 'pasting up' (literally doing just that with the bits and pieces that go to make a page). This is labour intensive and is a quite boring job if you have no connection with the text but is a deeply interesting and satisfying one if you have. It is quite likely that most of our groups, whilst increasingly contracting-out typesetting and printing to outside firms and presses, will want to keep control of their 'paste up'. In a very obvious sense this avoids the use of paid (unionised or otherwise) labour. Secondly, since very few of the Federation's groups have their own press (possibly only THAP and Commonword) a lot of the production process is actually contracted out. Usually, though, it is contracted to community presses, resource centres and other non-commercial (and frequently non-unionised) printers. The reasons for this are various but one obvious one is based on financial considerations. Very few, if any, of the groups can afford to take their books to large commercial printing companies. More than that, many of the non-commercial presses have taken a keen interest in the books they have printed; they have involved the writers and the compilers in seeing how the books are produced, have made suggestions for improving designs or choosing colour schemes for covers. This contrasts with the attitude of many commercial firms which is one of 'this is toytown stuff... normally we do runs of 50,000, three colours anyway, give it us here and we'll give you a ring when it's ready'.

Bridges over troubled waters

Again there are no easy answers. But one way forward is to seek state-grants either directly or indirectly (though a number of our groups would have strong reservations about the possible dependence and constraints implied by such a situation), in order to enable us to directly pay union rates or indirectly employ unionised labour through the community-based provision of printing and publishing facilities. It may also be that we have to talk to the unions concerned (we are, after all, on the same side) about the proper conditions under which this 'new technology' can be utilised in the area of working class publishing. We may, at some stage, have to think of resurrecting that old Labour movement weapon, the fair wage clause. We may even have to look anew at some of our own practices and ask just why it is that so many small, local organisations have so often, to put it politely, ignored or apparently been indifferent to organised labour. Just why is it that we appear to inhabit such different worlds?

There is, of course, one other area of importance with regard to our relationships with organised labour – the question of payment to writers. For working class publishing is radically different not only in creating new reading publics and new publishing possibilities for people who write, it also actively encourages new writers. It does this on the basis of regarding publishing as the last stage in the process of offering writers a means of sharing their experiences with others. It is not a commercial transaction whereby the publisher buys the manuscript from the writer in the hope of making a profit. No royalties are paid to authors. For writers who try to make a living by writing, and who might well be members of the TUC registered trade union for writers, the Writers' Guild, local publishing could be seen as another form of exploitation by undercutting the market. Local publishing might well give additional credence to the view that writing isn't really work, that it's just a recreation and people should feel grateful for being published, never mind paid.

Members of the Federation have had a meeting with a representative of the Writers' Guild at the TUC, organised by the TUC Education Office. We put our view on the new role of non-commercial local publishing in creating new writers and reading publics and they saw this new development and understood the reason for non-payment of authors. However, they were concerned that when people published by Federation groups were asked, as they often are, to read a few poems on radio, or make a television appearance, they should insist on payment at proper rates, otherwise this was genuinely undercutting union labour. When people active in the Federation have written for commercial companies we have encouraged them to join the Writers' Guild. Quite a few commercial publishers, particularly those of school books, have approached local publishing projects to reproduce poems or extracts from autobiographies for use in such things as school text books. A proper rate has always been asked for this right and the money, in most groups, passed directly to the writer as it is quite clear policy amongst Federation groups that, although writers do not get paid, copyright rests with them and so, therefore, do all subsequent reproduction rights.

This is just one small example of how the contradictions which we face might be dealt with – but the overall problem is a large and serious one. People in the Federation have often had a difficult and tenuous relation to mainstream trades unionism. If we really wish to be on the same side it's time we started building bridges. The very success of the movement has meant that we can no longer live on islands of alternative practices: our practice actively affects (and we hope will increasingly affect) people in the trade union movement. We need to recognise the seriousness of the contradictions that do exist and start to develop strategies for dealing with them.

Writers and communities

The writers' circle, or try anything once

A telephone rings.

Mavis: Hello. Bethnal Green Home for the Bewildered.

Shirley: Is that you Mavis?

Mavis: Oh, Shirley? Sorry, I picked that up from the kids and can't stop saying it now.

Shirley: Lucky I'm not in a call box, I'd have lost my money. Anyway, what did you think of last night?

Mavis: I quite enjoyed it Shirl, honestly. I was surprised, I didn't expect to.

Shirley: I told you didn't I? There was no reason to be embarrassed about your stuff. Some of their poems were a lot worse than yours.

Mavis: Did you think so? Oh thanks. I didn't like that long silence after I finished reading though. For a minute I thought I was going to be thrown out.

Shirley: Don't be daft. Who by?

Mavis: Well, I know it's silly of me, but when we first got in there I thought that big bloke next to the door was the bouncer. But of course later on when he read his story, I —

Shirley: Good, wasn't it? All that clever scientific stuff. I wouldn't have thought he had it in him. But then you can't go by appearances, I always say.

Mavis: No, especially when he kept on reading his comic all through your story.

Shirley: He didn't, did he?

Mavis: Oh, everyone else was listening Shirl. They were. Honest.

Shirley: Do you think they liked it?

Mavis: Oh, I'm sure they did.

Shirley: Are you? They looked a bit baffled to me.

Mavis: Well, you write very deep stuff Shirl and —

Shirley: I wish you'd stop calling me 'Shirl'. You know I can't stand it.

Mavis: Sorry. As I was saying — what was I saying? Oh yes. You write such deep stuff, I bet they'd never heard anything like it before.

Shirley: I think I was at least up to the standard of that tall sophisticated looking girl, don't you?

Mavis: The one who wrote that long sad poem about dying for love?

Shirley: OF love, not FOR it. Really Mavis, you never listen properly.

Mavis: W-ell, it was a bit over my head. She's a secretary you know, like you.

Shirley: Oh well. No wonder.

Mavis: No wonder what?

Shirley: Never mind, you wouldn't understand.

Mavis: I understood that other woman's poems, you know? The one all about babies and the family and all that. Nice, wasn't she.

Shirley: Oh yes. Motherly. Reminded me of my own mum actually.

Mavis: Funny you should say that. I was thinking the same thing. My mum keeps on losing her glasses and dropping things just like she did.

Shirley: And the convenor had such a job stopping her once she started, didn't he? I thought …

Mavis: The who?

Shirley: The one who was running it all. That quiet, studious looking fellow with the glasses.

Mavis: Oh him. Was he running it? I wondered what he kept knocking on the table for.

Shirley: What did you think he was doing — calling up the spirit world?

Mavis: Oh go on, Shirl — sorry Shirley. No one took any notice of him though, did they?

Shirley: No, they could have been better behaved, I must say. You could see he'd had a superior education to the others. Definitely a professional man.

Mavis: Get away. He was a plumber's mate. He told me in the pub afterwards.

Shirley: You're kidding. Well who was the one in the plumber's overalls then?

Mavis: Oh, he was a history teacher. They told me that too.

Shirley: Hm-mm… he did use a lot of basic Anglo-Saxon.

Mavis: Talking of language, what did you think of that blowsy woman? Talk about a dog's dinner. All that make-up and jewellery! Must have been fifty if she was a day and —

Shirley: Mutton dressed as lamb all right.

Mavis: — then she came out with that lovely gentle ghost story and not one four letter word in it.

Shirley: Mind you, she knocked back an awful lot of vodka afterwards, didn't she?

Mavis: They all drank like fish though, didn't they?

Shirley: I know, but I suppose you have to make allowances for creative people.

Mavis: Yes, I suppose you do...

Shirley: They didn't have anything else in common with each other at all really.

Mavis: No, they were all quite different, one way or another.

Shirley: – except for being Socialists.

Mavis: I didn't mention you voted for mother Thatcher last time, Shirley.

Shirley: Thanks.

Mavis: What do you think then? Shall we go again?

Shirley: We could still try the pottery class.

Mavis: Sounds a bit messy...

Shirley: Mm-mm. Of course there's still the Buddhist Meditation thing...

Mavis: Bit on the quiet side.

Shirley: Yes, they were sociable, that's true – for such an odd assortment of people.

Mavis: Odd. That's the word. That's what they had in common. No wonder we felt so much at home. Shirl? Shirley, are you still there? Hello...

Shirley: Mavis, I don't think I care for that insinuation.

Mavis: Ooh, I like that word – insinuation. Anyway, do you want to go next time? After all we've tried everything else – well almost – and it is free, after all.

Shirley: That's true, evening classes cost the earth. Well all right then, I'll see you.

Mavis: See you then, Shirley.

—Jean Archer

Local publishing is not simply a reflection or passive response to work received, but an intervention in people's lives, locally and nationally, which creates new confidence and abilities.

'Strong Words', the Durham and Tyneside group have described their experience in putting together the book *But the World Goes on the Same*. This was a collection of taped and written accounts of old and young people's lives as lived in a group of Durham pit villages which also included poems they had written. Once people got involved in taping and correcting their manuscripts they continued to write in forms quite separate from their original contribution to the book.

It has also been found at Centerprise in London that once people have been encouraged to talk about their lives on tape, and then edit their own transcript, they often carried on writing, having found the process an important way of reflecting and clarifying their experiences. Of the first six writers published by Centerprise, for example Ron Barnes, Vivian Usherwood, Christine Gillies, Dot

Starn, Arthur Newton, all carried on writing, not necessarily with a view to publication.

One of the community arts?

On more than one occasion, and in various places, groups active in the Federation have strongly resisted being defined or slotted into the category of Community Arts. The community arts movement, developed in the 1970's, was made up of, among others, mural painters, video makers and performers who wanted to practise their skills outside the conventional theatre and other such formal areas.

Many community arts projects have done very good work in working class districts, running festivals, initiating murals and so on. It is a professional movement, yet criticism – often from within – of the courses sometimes run on community arts can discourage those without a job-orientated interest. It is this element which makes the movement politically different from the worker-writer movement, committed as it is to the de-professionalisation of cultural production. At worst, some community arts are unreconstructed entertainment, pure clowning, with very little 'skill-sharing'.

The community arts movement has been financially marginalised by the creation of a Community Arts Panel by the Arts Council. Pressure has been taken off their various specialist panels for funding. Therefore all such projects are urged only to apply to that panel.

Greg Wilkinson's view was that the Arts Council have bought off the potentially oppositional cultural movements of the 1970's by setting up a cultural bargain basement at 105 Piccadilly and titling this the Community Arts Panel. The Federation of Worker Writers and Community Publishers has always in principle insisted that its financial needs should be addressed to the Literature Panel of the Arts Council of Great Britain. Similarly we have resisted all moves to reduce and counter-define the working class writing movement by labelling it 'community writing' as though this were some kind of second order activity compared with 'real' or 'national' writing.

New pressures

However, because we are writing and publishing within a society which has mystified publishing with assumptions and misunderstandings, there can be real difficulty in getting across to the people the ideals and cultural values which the new publishing groups use as a starting point. Consequently a number of those who have been published in this way have found problems arising from their involvement in writing. It has been the experience of several people on having had a book published that acquaintances assume that this has meant an enormous financial scoop for the writer, rather like a pools win. When told that no payment was involved, another response is to think that the writer was taken for a ride and that someone, somewhere, has pocketed a fair bit of cash. Yet another reaction is that all this activity is not 'real' publishing, which they associate with Habitat office suites, expense account lunches in Soho, television guest appearances and so on.

Even the writer may feel these pressures and begin to think that commercial publishing offers more, although we have to say that this is remarkably rare and that the common experience is a fierce loyalty to the local workshop and publishing project.

We have come to believe within the Federation that it is vital that we should develop alternative values and other contexts by which to celebrate the achievement of writing, in order that new writers may feel that there is proper recognition of all the effort and very hard work required to produce a manuscript.

One or two people initially published by one of the Federation groups have taken subsequent work to commercial publishers. There they have either been treated indifferently, or encouraged to become highly secretive about their writing – even told that it is bad to read work in progress to other people because it spoils the impact of publication – and so have actually been put off writing for its own sake or for the pleasure of others. Writing can become a possessive commodity.

But there are other causes of alienation too. When Ron Barnes published his second book, the highly regarded *Coronation Cups and Jam Jars* one relative wrote to the local newspaper, *The Hackney Gazette,* disowning the book and regretting that Ron Barnes had felt compelled to describe the very poor conditions in which his family had once lived. Ron Barnes, in his afterword to the book, describes meeting with people scornful of his autobiographical writings... 'Who more or less suggested that I was not the only one to experience distress in childhood, so why was it necessary to write that I did?' Their view was that it was only the 'special' people of the world who had license to recount their unique experiences in life.

The plain clothes writer

The writer who is honest to their experience treads a very sensitive path between truthfulness and what others feel to be a betrayal. Friends and relatives can regard writers as potential informers. Some people feel pressured to use a pseudonym when writing about such contentious issues as abortion or male chauvinist pub-culture in particular districts where such matters are thought best left undiscussed.

Roger Mills, who is active in the Federation, speaks of those who 'have been criticised by families and have met with hostility from relatives who feel exploited and exposed by a writer in their midst, a plain clothes writer at that, not even a copy of *The Complete Works of Shakespeare* under his arm as identification.

Susan Price, a supermarket worker before she began writing children's books, discusses this at length in an interview in the *Children's Book Bulletin:* 'Sometimes when I've gone into the local shops everyone is talking, but as soon as I go in then everything goes quiet. It was the same when I was the writer in residence at a teachers' training college. When I sat down the students, everybody would be talking away, and as soon as I sat down everybody stopped talking. There's nothing special about me at all'.

Things rarely reach these extremes, but the ambivalences about writers is still there; or we should say about people who, amongst other things, write.

On the whole those involved in local publishing and writers' workshops prefer to see themselves not as 'writers', but rather as people who sometimes write.

Pressure can also come from closer quarters than neighbours. The most common of these is the pressure on women from husbands to stay at home rather than go out to a writers' workshop – or any other kind of independent activity where different values operate from those at home. It does also occasionally work the other way round. Men are sometimes thought odd to be wasting their time on such an eccentric activity as writing. Some people keep secret their involvement in writing, telling nobody until this is revealed by publication.

Involvement in a group means much more than just going somewhere where you can discuss writing or work on a local history project. Other issues raise themselves. Why some people find anti-Irish jokes objectionable, why there should be equal representations of women as well as men in an anthology of working experiences, how the work of typing and making the coffees is to be shared out without assuming which sex is to do it, what should be done about publishing a story which contains a very convincingly drawn and sympathetic National Front member, even though the intention of the story is ultimately anti-racist. All these questions involve thinking through new ideas. Roger Mills again: 'People I know have been politicised through involvement in writers' groups. The evil of such things as racism and sexism have become clear to them in a way that all the isolated readings of *Socialist Worker* or *Spare Rib*, or other such publications given out like so much religious reading matter, could never have done'.

But the slow change in values, questioning of old assumptions and the growth of new friendships involves a distancing from the previous pattern of relationships. It would be wrong to suggest that the situation is critical, but for some people there have been real difficulties. These have been expressed by one writer in a very powerful poem:

And So a Different Mind

And so a different mind,
Nothing sudden or spectacular,
But smoothly it moves
Like a tide.
And leaving with each sweep upon the beach
Pebbles. Clear. Smooth. Precious.
No longer out of reach.

A betterment, yet in a way a hindrance.
But for everything in life, one has to pay.

Being one with those
Who wore those shabby clothes
And broken shoes.
But a different mind
Drives out the old,
Replaced by different views.

A greedy mind always wanting more,
And that alone will shut the door.
Yet I see a shaft of light.
And I hope.

Changing tone, changing speech,
To accommodate each you meet.
The price you pay each day.

> And one is lost
> In this urban mixture of different minds,
> Free minds, yet inclined to isolate.
> You try to choose from different views
> And different personalities.
> Friends act like enemies,
> And enemies, friends.
> The price you pay each day,
> To dare to think another way.
>
> —*Ron Barnes*

Pressures arise from becoming known as a working-class writer, both locally and nationally. Because of the still relative rarity of this phenomenon, the individuals who have become very active in this movement are often pressured into becoming 'representative' figures and taken up by the media. A book gets well reviewed in the local newspapers, this is picked up by local radio or even regional television. The working-class writer is portrayed almost as a freak. Once his or her name is known he/she becomes convenient. The person to interview or 'use' in any programme. They've got their working class writer, the one whose name and phone number they can remember, so that one gets over-exposed and exploited.

It was the experience of one writer, however, that having been invited to appear on local radio to talk about his writing he was turned away at the door and told to go round to the back entrance. He realised that the cause of this reaction was his working clothes which he was still wearing after a day's work on a nearby site.

Are writers special people?

Since writing has always been associated with a rare and deep intellectuality, people who have written very well about a range of subjects are assumed to be therefore knowledgeable about everything else, as well as being endlessly entertaining and witty at parties and in all ways singular and eccentric. This is due to the mass media's belief in the transferability of talent amongst 'well known' people. When someone becomes a famous actor or footballer their fame alone somehow renders their views in all fields equally significant. Not only is David Essex a popular singer, but he is invited onto chat shows and asked questions about South Africa and unemployment, as if his views had been given authority and weight by the mere fact that he is famous.

Again, from the Susan Price interview in the *Children's Book Bulletin:*

Q: *Has it created any problems for you being known locally as a writer?*

A: Yes, because people tend to think of writers as something which ordinary people can't be. They're supposed to be awe-inspiring but I know that I'm not awe-inspiring and I know I'm not particularly clever. It is all right with people you know, but when you meet people who have been told you are a writer they expect something very special. It's embarrassing because they expect you to be proof of a scintillating talent and you can't provide it because it's not there. It's a myth. A friend of mine always thought that writers lived in great big white houses on the tops of hills, with all the walls painted white, and they lay on a large white couch drinking vodka and occasionally went over to a white typewriter and typed a few words...

This attitude towards writers is not helped by the way in which the media present stories about working class writers. For example, Joe Smythe, a Manchester railway guard and member of the Commonword Writers' Workshop, was given a three-month Sabbatical by the NUR to produce a collection of poems *The People's Road,* in an excellent initiative by a trade union. It was published to commemorate the 150th anniversary of the Liverpool and Manchester Railway. When *The Guardian* ran a feature on its front page, mentioning this unusual venture, it did so under the headline of *'I wandered lonely as a guard'.* New writers are never judged or presented in their own right, but solely in terms of an established and different tradition. 'Is this Grimethorpe's answer to Shakespeare?' is the kind of local reporting which effectively trivialises very real and different cultural breakthroughs.

All these factors partly explain why many working class writers, song writers, comedians and playwrights have sought a platform for their ideas through the world of commercial entertainment rather than by means of 'Art and Letters'. People in working class areas are not entirely unused or surprised to hear of somebody in the locality entering showbiz, or finding out that some known writer came from round the corner. The fact that the writers no longer lived or even concerned themselves in their former working class environment might not shock them either, because like the showbiz star they've 'made it'. However, the practice of working class writers meeting together to become active in local affairs, writing poetry and prose that relate to current events, is still a novelty. The media turns ability and a yearning for expression into a show, a thing to be snatched from its birthplace and sold as genius, divorced from the environment that created it.

Finding a voice –
the struggle for
self-representation

Interesting, but...

Selling our books, talking about them, arguing their merits, we often come across the response (particularly from those with strong 'political' predilections) that they're 'quite nice really', 'enjoyable reading' and so on – but ultimately 'irrelevant'. 'Irrelevant' that is to 'real' political involvement (whatever that may be). If not 'coffee-table' stuff, the best it seems they can aspire to is tea and biscuits and old fogies wallowing in the 'good old days'. Harmless enough, by and large, but hardly of any great import. One of the main arguments running through this book is with this casual dismissal of ordinary working-people's writings as being of any relevance to the struggle for social change.

Just why that response should be so frequent and why we regard it as such a problem, particularly when made by those on the left, needs spelling out. One reason should be quite clear from the brief summary of the origins and development of the Federation, because that response of 'irrelevant' is the most colossal put-down imaginable of so-called ordinary people. It's surely a major problem for left political activists if their programmes and policies exclude working people's situations, needs and satisfactions as defined by themselves. Dismissal of this work by the Guardians of Culture is less surprising but still needs exposing, because it's a way of saying that everybody has a particular position in society and, by and large, should stick to it. Put crudely, if their writings are irrelevant, their expressions of themselves and their experiences of no interest, then so too are the writers. But of course in other respects *they* are of enormous interest, but of interest within certain closely defined social areas. They are of interest as producers (of material goods, of services, of taxes, etc.) or as consumers (of products, of politics, of TV programmes, etc.) – but not if they step outside these roles.

The fishermen who found no fish

Writing (i.e. communicating, making concrete certain social relationships, saying things publicly) is something beyond their means, best left to those well equipped to deal with such sensitive and sophisticated matters. As an ex-Chairman of the Arts Council put it, they:

... did decide to investigate the possibility that there might be reservoirs of talent which were being neglected because we did not know about them. —*The Guardian*, 28.12.81

But largely, it seemed, such reservoirs did not exist.

Which brings us to the third major reason for challenging that charge of 'irrelevance'. Just who constituted 'they' who decided to investigate the 'possibility' of 'reservoirs of talent'? It's doubtful whether anyone reading this book would know (unless of course, they happen to be attached to that particular institution) who made up that team of intrepid investigators going out into darkest Leeds or Manchester in search of undiscovered 'talent', or upon what criteria they searched for it. This is not the place for an assault upon the particular prejudices and predilections of the Arts Council, but it *is* the place for raising the central question of *representation*. How is it that certain people (in this case the Arts Council) have the right and power (as well as the purse strings) to decide what is and what is not 'good' writing, how are the criteria for such assessments established and by whom?

Put it another way, when was the last time you voted for a representative on the Arts Council (a body it might be said with £86 million at its disposal in the current year), or on any similar body? And why not? Because 'it's not important' and, anyway, they say, ordinary people wouldn't have the interest or the expertise to be involved in such esoteric pastimes, they're much better left to things they understand like beer, baccy and bingo.

The politics of representation

So what we're on about here is representation: who represents who, and in whose interests? One need go no further than the present state of national politics to see just how crucial this question of representation is. At the moment it's difficult to escape from questions about the nature and purpose of political representation in the battles between and within the major parties, about how people should be selected and to whom (and how) they should be responsible once selected for a particular office. And this is no esoteric question, because it's all about who has the power (in any particular sphere) to decide what happens and under what constraints they can use that power. Nor is it just a question of 'politics', it's about things like schools and parks and office blocks and businesses. It's about the continuous conflicts in all areas of life between those who claim to have power and authority and those who are on the receiving end.

We'd argue that much of the impetus within the Federation comes from a very deep-seated feeling amongst ordinary working people of powerlessness. Of not being represented, of not being properly represented, of being mis-represented.

On TV, for example, 'ordinary people' appear as studio audiences, as the objects of games-shows, as the ingredients of sit-coms, as the subjects of documentaries or even (occasionally) as the distant heroes of long dead histories. Not that TV, or any other major medium, ignores people; far from it – people, in this context, means pound notes. No, people aren't ignored, but they are represented in certain ways, under certain constraints.

Part of the justification is that it's only the 'experts', the controllers of TV stations or mass circulation newspapers, who really know firstly how to produce these items (like TV programmes or newspaper articles or novels or whatever), and secondly understand just what items ought to be produced. *They* know best and it's obvious that *they* know best, otherwise *they* wouldn't be in that position in the first place.

The TV Companies have in recent years made gestures in the direction of other, less exclusive, methods of production with programmes like 'Open Door' (though these are immediately labelled as 'minority' and therefore, again, 'irrelevant'). The great mass of people in this kind of set-up are simply there to be an audience. That, of course, imposes certain constraints upon the producers; they do, after all, need that audience to justify their productions in the first place. Nonetheless the whole system of producing (and distributing) cultural products is built upon the few producing for the many.

Self-representation

Against that, often in conscious opposition to it, the Federation and its affiliates are engaged in attempting to create a more open and democratic method of producing culture (in this case books). Just as there are autocratic and democratic ways of conducting politics or businesses or trade unions, so too are there democratic and auto-cratic ways of producing, making and distributing literature. What is important to us here is allowing people to represent themselves, of devising ways by which people, ordinary people, can organise and represent themselves. That is why we cannot divorce our methods of production (writing, discussing, criticising, editing, pasting-up and in every other way putting books together) from the 'finished products'.

Questions of representation and power do not only come up in relation to class, but also in relation to gender. In recent years women in many countries have begun to challenge the media's sexual stereotyping of them as pretty but dumb, incompetent everywhere but in the kitchen, the sexually deferential inferiors of men – stereotypes which contribute to their subordination.

But rather than simply respond with complaints of unfair treatment, the women's liberation movement, in its own films, books, music, and own magazines and journals, has presented positive accounts of women's own experiences. A similar struggle has happened amongst black people, particularly those living in ex-colonial settings, to resist and displace the crude imperialist ideologies of black ignorance and natural inferiority. These are not just abstract struggles or paper battles but massive social move-ments, attempts to construct different ways of relating to each other.

Haven't we been this way before?

Those with power have always tried to restrict access to, and control over, the means of communication. From the days when preachers were licensed by those in authority, from the days of the English Civil War when popular pamphleteers proved a threat to authorities of various political hues, the question of who should control, and under what terms, the dominant means of communication, has been of major interest to all Governments and to all ruling classes. But such concerns have also been those of the subordinate classes as well. It is no accident that the first radical working-class organis-ations in industrial Britain was the London *Corresponding* Society, with a very definite emphasis on that second term. Nor was it an accident when Government, in its efforts to crush such radical challenges, literally outlawed *corresponding*. Nor was it an accident, either, that many battles of the early nineteenth-century English working class movement were over the right to a free and unlicensed press.

Those past conflicts, like the present ones, were not just about communications in isolation. They were about the way in which particular societies should be organised, and about how social organisations should be depicted, and about who should decide what was right and what was wrong within those particular social organisations.

To put it another way, the struggle for freedom of speech has been inseparable from political and cultural struggle, and deliberate mis-representation has always been used to discredit radical movements. The early radicals, the Co-operators, the first trades unionists, the unemployed workers, were vilified in the press and in subsidised leafletting campaigns, as 'scum', 'the mob', and by other epithets, just as modern trades unionists were vilified in the media recently in the so-called 'winter of discontent'. Something called 'politics' cannot be divorced from something called 'communications' or the 'media'. Nor can it be divorced from something called 'culture'.

The struggles about representation, about resisting dominant views of working class life and the life of the nation, about demanding access to the means of spreading other and oppositional views, are always involved with political struggles, and this is where we place the movement of working class writing now developing. The particular character that this work takes is not direct opposition, not necessarily confronting in argument, but beginning to supplement or replace the dominant culture – creating, making space for, developing ways of distributing, the self-expression of working class people themselves, so that the dominant views will not have a free field. This emphasis too has a history which it is useful to be aware of.

This struggle over who should control, who should determine the nature of writing and publishing, has been going on for far longer than any of us have been around. It may be just that the recent movement of working-class writing and publishing has been more intense than its predecessors, but it also represents the re-emergence of a popular cultural and political tradition stretching back over at least the last two hundred years. Subordinate classes have rarely failed to make and organise their own culture, their own cultural organisations in (partial, at least) opposition to those of the dominant classes.

Earlier movements

The 18th century saw the publication of many small collections of verse by working people, often agricultural labourers, whose writing not simply portrayed a rural idyll but also a frequent sense of injustice at the conditions under which working people lived. In 1831 Southey published *An Essay on Uneducated Poets* which looked back at some of the self-taught poets of an earlier era: Ann Yearsley, milkmaid; John Taylor, Thames Waterman; James Woodhouse and John Bennet, shoemakers; Stephen Duck, farm labourer, and others.

Stephen Duck's case is described in Raymond Williams' recent *The Country and the City* as a very early example of the self-taught poet being taken up and patronised by people in the so-called higher classes and in the process having his early radical edge smoothed out. For the early Duck poems were full of the conditions of the labourers and their families in this rural landscape:

> Let those who feast at Ease on dainty Fare
> Pity the Reapers, who their Feasts prepare:
> For Toils scarce ever ceasing press us now;
> Rest never does, but on the Sabbath, show;
> And barely that our Masters will allow.
> Think what a painful Life we daily lead;
> Each morning early rise, go late to Bed;
> Nor, when asleep, are we secure from pain;
> We then perform our Labours o'er again:

Some years after being given an annual stipend of £30 through the offices of Queen Caroline (there was no Arts Council then) the tone and angle of perception had changed:

> Of blissful Groves I sing, and flow'ry Plains:
> Ye Sylvan Nymphs, assist my rural strains.

The nineteenth century witnessed a resurgence of independent literary culture (as well as whole new departures in working class cultural organisation) often closely associated with conflicts over political and trades union representation. Whilst such a tradition was continuous, as well as innovative, it had clear 'high spots', again frequently corresponding to political/social crises. Chartism, the mass working-class movement of the 1830's and 1840's, with its demands for full political representation and a People's Parliament, was not only accompanied by distinct cultural activities but also (perhaps more importantly) did not make, and refused to make, distinctions between the 'political' and the 'cultural'.

A distinct Chartist social world was constructed, based on a positive rejection of the existing social forms and institutions: radical bookshops, coffee shops, a vigorous press (which easily outsold the 'establishment' press) and reading rooms which often promoted public readings of news, of poetry, of serialised novels. It was not unusual for small groups to buy Chartist publications between them and to read these aloud together. There were writers' groups like the Poet's Corner in Manchester which boasted seventeen members when it published an anthology of its work in 1842. Indeed, a number of the best-known Chartists like Thomas Cooper and Ernest Jones were keen poets, and it is both significant and ironic that the only collection of Chartists' poetry ever published was published not in this country but in the Soviet Union.

In a similar vein there were a number of Chartist novels, often serialised in the thriving newspapers and journals of the movement. The Chartists believed that working-class people should produce their own literature, since established writers were incapable of creating a literature that gave full cognisance to the complex reality of everyday working-class life and politics.

The defeat of Chartism in the late 1840's brought with it a period of apparent 'calm', but the revival of the independent working-class movement in the 1870's also produced a new literature and a new audience for literature. The early working-men's clubs which proliferated in the last three decades of the nineteenth century were part and parcel of a widespread revolt against middle class supervision and tutelage in political parties, trades unions, factories as well as clubs. These clubs often included in their programmes readings of Shakespeare, Byron, Shelley as well as the poetry of the elder Chartists and of club members themselves.

The independent working-class movement of the 1870's to the First World War, like its predecessors, was not only highly self-educated politically (creating such educational organisations as the Central Labour College and the Plebs League) but maintained a high degree of interest in science, philosophy and literature. It also found itself in increasing competition with and opposition to the infant mass entertainment industry and state education. The decline, or rather the transmutation, of working-men's clubs into branches of the entertainment industry (under the impact of centralised booking agencies and the developing 'star' system), clearly demonstrated the difficulties, if not the impossibility, of maintaining a totally independent existence.

More recent times

The 1930's was a significant era for working-class writing though this took a different form from that of earlier periods. At the same time the tradition of working-class education survived and in some cases even thrived, despite efforts to undermine it (for example by the 'tutelage' of the WEA).

The worker-writer movement of the 'thirties was a diffuse cultural and political association which included the documentary film movement, the Workers' Film Movement, the Workers' Theatre, the various Labour Party sponsored sports organisations, workers' painting groups such as the Ashington miners, documentary writing projects such as those initiated by Mass Observation, Unity Theatre and literary initiatives such as *Left Review* and *New Writing*. Culture was clearly as much a battlefield as ever – the positive alarm with which showings of Eisenstein's *Battleship Potemkin* were viewed in some quarters could be seen as ludicrous were it not for the fact that present film societies owe the restrictions under which they operate to just such alarm at uncontrolled access to 'political' material – hence the peculiarly British policy of pricing them out of the market through high membership fees.

In the 1930's the characteristic publishing process was very much controlled by sympathetic middle-class intellectuals like John Lehmann and George Orwell, who encouraged working-class people, particularly men, to write down their experiences, either in direct autobiography or fictionalised form. The system was one of patronage, well intentioned but liable to founder in the case of personal animosity between patron and writer.

Work of great significance was also published in this period by members of the Women's Co-operative Guild. *Maternity* in 1915 and *Life as We Have Known It* were both encouraged into print by Virginia Woolf.

Many of the best-known working-class autobiographies and novels of the 'thirties, such as B.L. Coombes' *These Poor Hands*, Willy Goldman's *East End My Cradle*, the early writings of Jack Common and George Garrett, are dedicated to Lehmann or some other patron. The magazines of that period, *New Writing* and *Left Review*, encouraged working-class writing but from a centralised and commissioning point of view. The Communist Party played no small part in encouraging the publication of working-class autobiographies like Phil Piratin's *Our Flag Stays Red* and Lewis Jones' *Cwmardy* and *We Live*, though the emphasis lay very heavily on novels and autobiographies, with very little attention to poetry, perhaps only Idris Davies, an ex-South Wales miner, being the exception.

Nor was it only a question of publishing. One of the major organisational breakthroughs was the massively successful Left Book Club, with its extraordinary output of books on international and domestic questions, and network of discussion groups and popular lectures. At the time this was seen as a major threat, not just by the right (with its Right Book Club) but also by the Labour Party, which went so far as to proscribe membership of the Club. Ernest Bevin, for one, felt its real purpose was 'to undermine and destroy the Trade Unions and the Labour Party as an effective force'.

1945 and after

This profuse and varied cultural growth was interrupted (to put it mildly) by the advent of the Second World War. Even so, within service life, adult education classes, discussion groups and so on, kept alive many of the pre-war issues.

It's also worth mentioning that cultural deprivation – in the sense of the wide spread of low standards of literacy and general education – was the shock revelation of mass conscription and mass 'screening' in the Second World War, just as malnutrition and physical deprivation had been in the First.

The Army Bureau of Current Affairs was often criticised from the right for its activities in facilitating topical discussions. Indeed to many on the right it seemed as if that massive Labour landslide in 1945 owed a lot to such 'cultural' and 'educational' activities. As the right-wing cultural magazine *New English Review* saw it in 1946:

This new post-war Parliament can fairly claim to be representative. It is the legitimate fruit of much earnest endeavour. Classes, discussion groups, summer schools... book clubs and bureaux of current affairs, have brought it into being. A vast wash of words, both written and spoken, has prepared the way for its coming, and now it has come. Leftism has arrived and is installed in Westminster.

Clearly other forces had played a part in this development but nevertheless this serves as eloquent testimony to a decade of cultural activity and organisation.

It also heralded a cultural counter-attack. It was not the war which brought to a halt the working-class movement of the 'thirties but, ironically, the new Labour Government.

There had been signs before the war that large sections of the Labour Party's leadership were at best indifferent, and at worst hostile, to the self-education traditions which had characterised the early working-class movement and to more recent forms of cultural politics. When the Labour Party came to power in 1945, committed to a programme of economic and social reconstruction, it quickly became evident that cultural reconstruction was not part of that agenda. Clear, too, that that process of reconstruction was going to be organised from above. Raymond Williams in *Politics and Letters* remembered this moment very clearly:

I thought that the Labour Government had a choice: either for reconstruction of the cultural field in capitalist terms, or for funding institutions of popular education and popular culture that could have withstood the political campaigns in the bourgeois press that were already gathering momentum. In fact there was a rapid option for conventional capitalist priorities – the refusal to finance the documentary film movement was an example. I still believe that the failure to fund the working-class movement culturally when the channels of popular education and popular culture were there in the forties became a key factor in the very quick disintegration of Labour's position in the future.

Just as important was the deliberate cultural counter-offensive, often tied in with the politics of the emerging Cold War. As the Cold War took hold, many of those who had been most deeply involved before found themselves ostracised as Communists or 'fellow travellers'. Thus in 1948 a three-day conference on the state of contemporary Theatre, chaired by J.B. Priestly, addressed by Stafford Cripps (Chancellor of the Exchequer), was boycotted by the entire West End theatrical establishment on the grounds that the organising secretary, Ted (now Lord) Willis, was a Communist.

That small world's ending

Throughout the fifties, when real gains in comfort and pay disguised the lack of change in power relations between classes, the slogan was that class culture was dying a natural death: 'We're all middle class now'. Class culture seemed to be succumbing to commercially organised mass culture. Intellectuals who had come from working-class homes worked at recording the culture of the communities of their childhoods in works like Hoggart's *The Uses of Literacy,* Willmott and Young's *Family and Kinship in East London,* and Jackson's *Working Class Community;* but the pressure seemed to be to record them before they disappeared. This notion has fed into the dismissal of reminiscences and local histories as un-political. If these cultures don't exist, if they no longer have any power to rally and unite people and to form the springboard for action, then indeed there is a political problem of a kind not dealt with by the continuity of the left's sources, programmes and rhetoric.

That is a problem too big for us to tackle within this book: all we can do is point to the fact that if spaces are made to listen to people — not the conditional space of the interview but spaces in which they can develop what they want to say — then what is to be heard is not a set of illusions about living in a classless society. The changes are real and large and they are reflected in the writing. Mary Casey's poem, 'The Class Game', is written about a world in which it is possible to pretend or to be confused about class positions, but it is still strong and challenging.

The Class Game

How can you tell what class I'm from?
I can talk posh like some,
With an 'olly in me mouth,
Down me nose, wear an 'at not a scarf,
With me second hand clothes.
So why do you always wince when you hear
Me say "Tara to me Ma" instead of "Bye Mummy dear"?
How can you tell what class I'm from?
'Cos we live in a corpy, not like some,
In a pretty little semi, out Wirral way,
And commute into Liverpool by train each day.
Or did I drop my unemployment card,
Sitting on your patio (we have a yard)?
How can you tell what class I'm from?
Have I a label on me head, and another on me bum?
Or is it because my hands are stained with toil,
Instead of soft lily-white with perfume and oil?
Don't I crook me little finger when I drink me tea,
Say toilet instead of bog when I want a pee?
Why do you care what class I'm from?
Does it stick in your gullet, like a sour plum?
Well mate! A cleaner is me mother,
A docker is me brother,
Bread pudding is wet nelly,
And me stomach is me belly,
And I'm proud of the class that I come from.

—*Mary Casey*

Nor are the celebrations, in prose and verse, of 'that small world's ending' passive or uncritical. There are aspects of the old world, and of its working-class cultures, which everyone is glad to see the end of; and also there is a criticism of the lives that have replaced them in the re-creations of the human support (and comedy) that the 'small world' made possible. To write is to record and assert the humanity of those who write – as is the case with any social action: to build, to entertain, to play, to organise. It should be clear that the continuation of this among the other cultural traditions is of the first importance in this decade when 'the end of ideology' itself looks like a brief illusion, the power struggle within society hardens again, and the humanity of the powerless is again discounted.

Small world

Outside the fair at Ardwick Green
hot potatoes from the hot-potato man
stay like a taste for the old exotic,
The hot-potato man, the organ grinder,
the knockerupper thieving dreams,
the donkeystone with dollyblue man,
the foggy tram conductor's cough,
the policeman with his street wide feet,
the local burglar with apprentice,
the man who fought Len Johnstone
the length of Brunswick Street,
Preaching Billy Arbuthroyd in flight
from nightwork husbands,
the born lights of singing pubs
that small world's ending.

—*Joe Smythe*

Writing, culture and class

Socialist or working class?

Our description and analysis of current working class writing has, so far, emphasised organisation. We have seen how the movement organises itself internally and how it is connected, on a much wider scale, to issues of self-representation within working class experience. We will later examine the way in which this challenges certain pre-conceptions about literature and also some of the principles on which cultural policies are founded and executed. In doing so we will be dealing with the large and unwieldly areas of *culture, literature, class, language* and *education*. It is important and necessary to do this and, as long as we avoid wilful obscurity, to do so with the help of abstract thinking. The energy which working class writing currently exemplifies and generates probably exists collectively more than individually, and its importance is certainly collective rather than individual. At the same time, however, there is a fundamental importance carried by individual acts of writing. This dialectic between the individual as writer and as workshop member, and between individual workshops in themselves and as the basis of an expanding national movement, lies behind many of the debates which continue to influence the direction of growth of the movement. Issues that have been particularly engaging recently include such arguments as whether the movement is 'socialist or working class' and questions about whether the concerns of women and feminists, in relation to writing, cut across or remain within traditional class boundaries − a debate which has recently been sharply argued in the Federation's own journal *Voices*. These questions bear on the act of writing − what subjects are written about and in what ways − and whether these are, can be or ought to be, distinctively working class. At the point where these concerns encounter the Establishment, either educational or cultural, issues of language and forms of writing invariably appear.

But, to begin from the beginning, we need to look first at the predominant themes and forms of the writing with which we are concerned.

What are we writing about?

Gerry Gregory, an English teacher who has written about Federation publications and their use in schools, has produced a breakdown of the common themes occurring in workers' writing and community publishing from the late 1960's onwards. He makes the important observation that '... the range of themes is as wide as in any comparable body of work... all the big, perennial themes that all speakers and writers at times try to confront (childhood, becoming adult, marriage, war and peace, death etc.) are represented.

One important thing shown by Gerry Gregory's analysis is the continuity with what others regard as 'real' writing. Federation writing is importantly and dramatically *different*, but that difference is *within* the broad limits of cultural experience, not outside of it. Any element of discontinuity with traditional cultural expectations comes into play because themes are represented by and for a working class viewpoint, and predominantly those of the inner-city. Thus themes become distinctive or common to forms of remembered or contemporary working class experience.

Such themes usually begin with a strong memory of childhood and street culture, street games, going to the markets, stealing from the markets, home life – especially marriage relationships and physical conditions. Home life experiences naturally remain in people's memories in very deep ways, more so if there was a pattern of heavy drinking by the father – often a response to living and working conditions; domestic violence does loom large in many autobiographies as does devotion to self-sacrificing mothers.

School experience is often remembered as authoritative, dull and even brutish, yet often with the memory of the one outstanding teacher who took an interest. Sometimes such a teacher was a socialist, a pacifist, or in some other way at right angles to their own class background and professional status. Many remember starting work in very harsh conditions, being treated miserably, sometimes learning a trade, often moving from job to job in the hope of finding what they really wanted to do. Women recall going into 'service', not daring to wear a wedding ring if they had an office job. More recent experiences include redundancy, automation, losing the right to exercise your skills, being made to produce had work at the insistence of the employer.

Against these harsher memories are others of a happier nature
– of mutual help within the factory and within the street, playing
tricks, having a laugh, making something out of nothing, materially
and emotionally, patching and mending, scrimping and saving, not
giving in, not going under, keeping a tidy house, making sure
everybody in the house contributed to the domestic chores and
economy. There was backyard cultivation and husbandry, allot-
ments, having to eat your favourite pet rabbit for Sunday dinner (or
retiring to the bedroom in tears), or going hungry to the point of
malnutrition on wartime rations.

And then there were memories of relationships with the authorities; mostly conflict, going up to the Assistance Board, or the
Guardians, having to hold onto your tongue as the Receiving
Officer told you to sell your one cheap clock before any financial
assistance could be forthcoming, being told by the Unemployment
Board (often made up of local employers) that one hadn't really
looked for work, giving a 'piece of one's mind' back at contemp-
tuous head teachers, patronising welfare visitors, social security
snoopers, being batoned by the police on unemployment demon-
strations and abused as 'parish-fed bastards'. For some there were
court appearances, approved schools or Borstals, Dr Barnardo's
and other children's institutions.

Obviously the last war affected many people profoundly – as
evacuees, as parents, as members of the forces, as the ones who dug
out the bodies after the air-raids. '... Everything went up; no
houses, no man, no mother and no boy. We picked up three
dustbins full of pieces out of the rubble. The only way to identify
where they were was the dampening dust and clouds of flies... war is
bestial and no solution to the world's problems. War is failure, the
culminating failure of failure'. (Stanley Rothwell's *Lambeth At
War.* Nostalgia? Political naivity? Local?) Many people had to
think about what was happening to them as a result of the war and,
consequently, there were many 'awakenings', a growing realisation
of, and involvement in, political and trade union struggles. In more
recent years housing struggles and rent strikes have been particularly important reasons for solidarity and political awareness. The
rise of the modern women's liberation movement has given many
older women who have fought the system even more confidence to
confront sexism with more emotional and moral support. Much new
writing is coming from black people whose lives have been radically
changed by living in a very different, and often hostile society.
Women's writing, together with black people's writing, is one of the
strongest areas within the Federation's recent growth. People are
also very keen to write or talk about new interests or commitments;

to painting, to writing itself, to a newly discovered interest in history, to new relationships and friendships, particularly between the generations. Indeed one of the strongest features of all Federation activities is the enormous age range of people involved, at local and national level.

These then are the predominant themes and concerns of the work we are writing about. But we need also to consider the question of the forms through which these are expressed. In the process of language becoming literature, form, as an organiser of content, becomes a critical issue.

If we look at a simple miscellany of writing, some examples of which follow, we will realise that we are talking about a great variety of forms which express a real diversity of experience.

Storytelling

At night time, about say eight o'clock in the night everybody close in. Especially if you live in the country. If you are in the country, the country part is always dark.

So, by eight o'clock everybody is in. So you and your family sit down and sometimes your mother sit down and she start to tell you lots of stories.

So we always say, "Mummy, stop! Don't say it yet, until we go and get ready." We go out side and we wash our feet and face and hands and come in and sit down. We take up everything that we're supposed to take in, so that we don't have to go back there while she's telling us the story. Because we always afraid, you know.

Deadly scared of some of them scary stories.

—M.C., from 'Milk River'

A Way Out

It was late at night
when I realised
I should have left a note for the milkman
for two loaves for the children's dinners
the next day at school.
The trouble was
I could not spell loaves,
and as my husband was asleep
I had to write the note on my own.
After four attempts
it went as follows.
"Milkman. Can you leave me a cut loaf. Thank you.
P.S. Make that two."

—Write First Time

English literature – GCE

Two dozen pupils
Dissect the set texts
Relentless hands
Ripping apart the delicate flowers
Petal by petal
To learn
How to understand beauty

—Savitri Hensman, from
'Hackney Writers' Workshop'

The prisoner's tale

By the end of that week he was snarling and splitting bullets. When
he got home after that last shift, his wife wasn't home. He wasn't
unduly worried, perhaps she was shopping or visiting relatives. It
was Saturday so he backed a few horses and went for a drink. He
went to the prison officers social club as the nasty screws can only
drink with their own kind for fear of reprisals from ex-cons. He
arrived home at four that afternoon, the worse for drink. In fact,
stoned out of his crust. His wife wasn't there. He was more than a
little annoyed. He stormed through the house shouting her name
and banging doors. It still didn't dawn on him that she was gone. He

fell into a sodden sleep. He awoke at four that morning cold and aching in every joint, he realised then that she had gone. He checked all the wardrobes and confirmed his fears. He went to bed with a troubled mind. Sunday morning he felt terrible, nothing had changed, but he didn't dwell on for too long, he was back on the day shift. All the way to work he was blind to all but his problem, never once in his reverie did he consider that he might be wrong.

On the top landing of the jail there is a gothic arch which is vaguely reminiscent of a cathedral. Oblong stood there steely eyed looking nothing like a Bishop. You can bet your life that a man like that, wearing steel toe cap boots in the mood he was in would have to kick something, and Joey's cell was on that landing. He was the catalyst without ever knowing why. Joey was really pissed off. His woman had sent him a 'Dear John' she had said she could wait no longer, and was going to London to live with somebody else. A man who had told her he could be a loving father to Joe's son. Joe was sick with rage. He paced his cell in silence breathing heavily through flared nostrils, his mind afire with violence and hatred.

Tea-time the bell's clanger echoed through the lofty prison wing, woke the sleepers and grated on raw stripped nerve ends.

Joe didn't want any food, he didn't have the stomach for it, McKenna, his cell mate was worried. He didn't know what was wrong with Joe, but as a veteran convict he could easily guess. He left Joe in the cell and went for his food. All the time he stood in the food queue he was thinking about Joey's reaction to the letter he received, how he'd paced up and down constantly, and he'd heard the occasional sob catch in his throat. McKenna knew it to be an explosive situation and, handy though he was in a fight, he was really scared of Joe. He recognised the berserker's rage in Joe's demeanour. A thing seldom seen but never forgotten. He knew he'd have to talk it over with Joe before things got out of hand. He also knew he'd have to take care because Joe might take exception to meddling of any description, and may even take McKenna's head off. He found himself at his cell surging with adrenalin super-charged with fear.

The food was the same slop they had eaten the previous Sunday and had been every preceding Sunday by thousands of men for the past ninety years with barely any variation at all, but McKenna didn't complain, he ate it all without tasting any, all the while he ate he watched Joe, who was sat on his bunk with his head in his hands, out of the corner of his eye. His 'meal' finished, he rolled a cigarette and held his tin out to Joe, who didn't notice until he tapped it lightly on the iron bed head. He took it without a word and rolled up mechanically whilst looking straight ahead.

McKenna spoke, 'D'ya wanna talk about it Joe?'
Joe looked up startled, as if he'd thought himself alone.
'Talk about what?' McKenna was wired through with agitation;
'Whatever it is that's bugging ya.' Joe turned to face the wall again.
There was a sigh of apathy in his voice, 'No, I don't wanna talk
about it'.
'Well I just thought maybe I could help you.'
Joe turned to look at him, and there was a definite breaking
point in his voice. 'Unless ya got the key to that fuckin' gate out
there you can't help me.' McKenna just nodded, he knew he could
take it no further, so he lay on his bed and read his book.
Exactly one hour after tea, Oblong began unlocking for slop
out. He had a go at just about everybody he could, with the
exception of Billy Markham (who was known as the animal, and
wouldn't think twice about throwing a screw off the top landing)
and then he came to Joe's cell.
'Slop out, leave your tea trays by the door.'
Joe didn't hear him, he was still on his back with his face in his
hands.
'Hey! Black Beauty! slop out.' There was a savage stinging taunt in
his voice which went completely unnoticed by Joe. Seeing his words
had no effect he raised his voice, 'Shape yourself you stupid black
bastard!' Joe couldn't fail to hear that. He looked up at Oblong as
though he'd noticed something nasty stuck to his shoe, but said
nothing, picked up his pot and took it to the ablutions. On his return
he was surprised to find Oblong still there.
'Where's your tea-tray, Sambo? You haven't ate it have you?'
There was a savage tone to his voice. McKenna knew it was going to
go off, when you've seen it as often as he you learned to read all the
signs. The air was heavy with static charged tension. Joe squared up
to Oblong, he'd had enough.
'I didn't get no tea. It's fuckin' shit anyway.'
'What did you say, nigger?'
'I said it's fuckin' shit anyway, white trash!'
Oblong went quite hysterical shouting, 'What did you call me?'
and tried to push Joe into his cell, he'd have stood more chance than
a brick wall. Then Joe hit him. His fist didn't move more than six
inches, Oblong went sprawling against the hand-rail and nearly over
it. He rushed Joe then flailing like a windmill. Joe give him a couple
of buffeting blows that started blood flowing and constellations
behind his eyes. He knew he had no chance at hand to hand.
Backing away he drew his truncheon, an eighteen inch penis of
black ebony. The first blow glanced off Joe's skull and smashed his
right ear. Joe was still standing. More in fear than hatred, Oblong

dealt repeated blows to Joe's head until Joe went down, his head was red ruin. He was free from all his troubles then. Oblong stood there, gasping like a steam engine. The other screws came running up then, and knelt down checking Joey's pulse etc.

Oblong was hysterical. 'Look what the bastard did to me!' His voice was a high pitched whine. 'Just look what he did.' He was pointing to one of several bruises, and the blood on his shirt front. McKenna looked at him with a mixture of pity and contempt. He walked one step to the table and picked up the crumpled letter. But he'd seen it all before. He shook his head sadly. Yes, he'd seen it so many times that it ceased to make sense. Poor Joey.

He was still alive, just a little scrambled upstairs, forgot his name sometimes, things like that, but he'd be released eventually to play a useful part in society. Oblong was suspended on full pay for three months until the board, formed by prison commissioners to investigate those who administer to the prison, concluded that 'the officer used justifiable means to subdue a violent prisoner'.

—*Sammy Tierney, Commonword*

Definitions of a cell

a small room, as in a prison
or monastery; a small cavity;
the simplest unit in the structure
of living matter; a division
of a voltaic or galvanic battery;
a small room, as in a prison,
where the simplest units in the
structures of a Mr. J. Kelly and
a Mr. L. Towers were murdered.

—*Nick Ripley, Commonword*

A kind of socialism

The men didn't give their wives all their wages either. They used to have what they called 'keepy back', money which they used to hide from their wives. Men used to get up to some amazing tricks to hide the money. Men coming home from the pit would have to bath, take their clothes off and keep half a gold sovereign in their hand. They'd wash themselves with their hand in a fist. They'd hide them in their carbide lamps, all sorts of things. There'd be hell to pay when the woman found out but, in these villages, you weren't a man if you didn't have some 'keepy back'.

—*George Alsop in 'Changing Times'*

No escape, 1979

1920's Media: These burns and woods and we, like solid rocks
               can easily withstand the thunderclap,
               can easily survive the frantic shocks
               of transient mobs. That life-giving sap
               of ancient vintage dies then thrives again,
               again and again fed by faith in kings.
               As sure as warmth and sunshine follow rain
               the people of this land accept these things.
               Yet, mercy is the hallmark of such strength
               those who erred will not feel vengeance done;
               that we shall never go to such a length
               is certain as our empire greets the sun.

Memory: But it was never like that...
               I am on a train heading south and watch
               the telephone wires race towards the ground
               to be swept up by the oncoming poles always
                    oncoming
               In the other track is trough of water, mile on mile
               Uncle Will explains in a broad Bedlington Brogue
               the engine lets its gob down, scoops up water,
                    inhaling food.
               Men carry distemper to London, 200 miles.
               We were to be the Kenties now,
               the erring, nudged off the doorstep
               by the benevolence of northern owners.

Echo: The benevolence of northern owners
               is in a blacklist, which you may think grows
               inside a man's head like some parasite.
               Or, do you think it's something deep and stagnant
               like a dull pool that only comes to life
               when poked or stirred? It's nothing of the like
               that can be labelled rancour or revenge.
               'Tis something sharp and clinical and cool,
               incisive, decisive, always ready:

a simple list of names for reference
with which the keen eyed gaffer prosecutes,
robbing a man of heritage and roots.

Memory: At Victoria in the rain my father laughed:
this is the railway of the Sunny South Sam!

*—Dennis Lawther in 'But The World Goes On
The Same: Changing Times in Durham Pit Villages'*

Under Oars

Here is an account of one night's work with a drunken man. I was
sent to Victoria Dock to be second hand up with a barge laden with
seventy tons of wheat to French's Mill at Bow Bridge. This meant
going up the River Lea, or as it is termed, Bow Creek, which is tidal,
the entrance being just above Victoria Dock...

We are nearing Westminster Bridge and both of us are aft
keeping her straight, as the tendency is for craft to come broadside
to a wind. There is good way on her so pointing her to the centre of
number four arch we take the middle. Attention of the lad was
called to the cruel looking buttress here, edges like knives, shapes
similar to a ship's ram; the lower the tide the more pronounced ram
for awkward or unlucky people. A bundle of straw is hanging
suspended in the centre of the arch. I explain this is a signal that
repairs are being done at this spot to the bridge. When under the
arch I gaze up into the staging; there is a painter pausing in his work
looking down at our barge shooting through. Cupping both hands I
yell so that the echoes ring (most bridges will produce an echo):
'What stinks worse than a painter?' A reply was expected, but not
the reply, 'A dirty little barge boy!' He won. Here was I, in charge,
with a new apprentice, patent to all observers, being actually
considered by another workman a dirty little boy. I suffered from an
inferiority complex for the next five minutes.

To regain my spirits I demonstrate to the lad how an oar should
be handled. He is shown how to carry this from end to end of the
craft, blade in water, speedily and safely, and, how to throw it 'for
'ard' for steering. It is essential for this to be smartly and correctly
accomplished. An oar can easily take charge of its owner, especially
when the craft has good headway going through the water, such as
when entering slack water from the tideway, similar in fact to a
novice in a row boat 'catching a crab'. The 'feel' of how to handle an
oar, in this case 28 feet long, comes by practice. A real smart
operation is to shift the oar from the rowing tack of crutch to the

opposite side in one movement around the bow. This is done by walking smartly 'forward' with the oar, blade tilted, causing the blade to be parallel with the handle, then placing the point of balance on the bitt head or fore post, weighing down on the handle, and with a semi-circular movement – hands, arms and feet working in unison – the oar is flung say from port side to starboard. This may appear a lot of words, but I can assure anyone who may be interested in river work that these essentials formed an important item of 'under oar' work.   —*Harry Harris, from 'Under Oars'*

In a hard winter

'*A low level of heating allowance should be incorporated in the basic scale rates, and heavy heating costs should be met by the SBC only in "extreme rare cases",'*   —*From* Social Assistance: a review of the supplementary benefit scheme in Great Britain (*Department of Health and Social Security*)

It costs money to be old
Lucky he who has trousers without holes
Lucky he who goes to bed
Having fed

Soon, oh soon
They'll have measured our life,
Crumbled in a crematorium's iron spoon
But before this consummation
Sons and daughters of this wealthy nation
Have to measure their untreasured life in hypotherms
Of no-gas, no-paraffin, nor anything that burns –
    It costs money to be old
    It costs money not to die of cold

Shall I dare, oh, shall I dare
Walking down the 13 storey stair
Shall I undertake a visit
Where the lady says: 'What is it?
'I am busy. You are late.
'Did you think that North Sea Oil
'Is for burning in your grate? –
'or for drink?'

– 'Lady, I have wept and fasted, wept and prayed
'Without drink or any vices
'Without cakes or buns or ices
'I am bleeding morning, afternoon and night,
'From a deep financial crisis' –
– 'Really?' – flicking through the file with
    outstretched finger
Making sure I don't malinger
(Don't malinger being old)

And here comes the ready, formulated phrase:
– 'Sorry, you will have to wait
'Anyway, it isn't up to me
'Why not go and have a cup of tea?' –

I am Lazarus, frozen to be dead
Stretched across the heatless floor...
Sorry, mate, I couldn't make the door

—Lotte Moos, from 'Time to Be Bold'

Harrassment

One evening me a com from wok,
And a run fe ketch de bus,
Two police start fe run me dung,
Just fe show how me no have no luck,
Dem ketch me and start to mek a fus,
Say a long time dem a watch how me,
A heng, heng round de shop

Me say me? What? heng round shop?
From morning me da a wok,
Me only jus stop,
An if onoo tink a lie ma a tell,
Go an go ask de manager

Dem insisted I was a potential tief,
And teck me to de station,
Anyway dem sen and call me relations,
Wen dem com it was a big relief,
Fe se som one me own color,
At least who woulda talk and laugh wid me

An me still lock up in a jail,
So till me people dem insist dat
Dem go a me wok to get som proof,
The police man dem nearly hit the roof,
Because dem feel dem was so sure,
That it is me dem did have dem eyes on,
Boy, I don't know what's rong,
With this babylon man,

Dem can't tell one black man from de other one
Anyway, when we reach me wok place,
Straight away de manager recognise me face,
And we go check me card fe se me dis clock out

So me gather strength and say to de coppers,
Leggo me onoo don't know wey onoo on about,
You want fe se dem face sa dem a apologise,
But when me look pon how
Me nearly face disgrace,
It mek me want fe kus and fight,
But wey de need, in a babylon sight,
If you right you rong,
And when you rong you double rong

So me a beg onoo teck heed,
Always have a good aleby,
Because even though you innocent,
Someone always a try,
Fe mek you bid freedom goodbye

—Fred Williams, 'Moving Up'

Knowhow & wisdom

There is 'knowhow' and there is wisdom,
these are worlds apart,
For 'knowhow' lives within the head
and wisdom in the heart.
If the trees of science
are not tended with great care,
the bitter fruit of intolerance
will bloom profusely there.
Planners with great 'knowhow',
will bulldoze the friendly street
replacing them with warrens

Tall towers of concrete.
Splitting friendly neighbours
into isolated cells,
Then bring in the psychiatrists
to hush the lonely yells.
They will gird the country lanes
into an asphalt yoke
isolating the country
from the country folk.
They will mix their noxious lotions
to further their own ends
polluting all about us
with their baneful blends.
They have tamed the mighty atom
and caged it just in case
they need its grim precision
to wipe out the human race.
The arrogance of 'knowhow'
can crush the human heart
When knowhow rules compassion
wisdom will depart.
And the humble individual
will fall along the way
Mid data and computers
if knowhow rules the day.

—*Mary Casey*

The forms of writing

As varied as the themes themselves are the forms through which writers realise and work on those themes. It is true, of course, that certain forms predominate are even, as in the case of autobiography, taken to be characteristic. Autobiography, particularly as a form of history writing, has generated a certain amount of controversy. Before we look in detail at those issues let us consider the occurrence of other forms within the writing.

Why no novels?

One of the most striking differences today between contemporary worker writers and those of earlier periods is the absence of novels. Arguably there has only been one contemporary novel produced from within the FWWCP, *The Gates*, a fictional account by two East London teenagers of their experiences in a succession of truancy schemes and maladjustment schools, which was published by Centerprise in 1974. This is in marked contrast to the 1930's when the novel was by far the most important means of representing working class life and experience. That era produced such important books as Greenwood's *Love on the Dole*, Walter Brierley's *Means Test Man*, John Somerfield's *Mayday*, Lewis Jones' *Cwmardy* and *We Live* and James Barkes' *Major Operation*. Perhaps this is because people no longer feel so obliged by family and neighbourhood pressures to fictionalise their own experience and are now much happier to relate them directly as autobiography. Clearly many of the earlier novels were based on real experiences, lightly fictionalised, to distance the writer from the events and traumas of the characters and their times.

Most of the 1930's novels were dedicated to a patron, usually a left wing intellectual. One such was John Lehmann, who bore the responsibility of publishing and who, occasionally, encouraged or financially supported the writing. As this system of patronage has now disappeared the difficulties of sustaining creative, imaginative work over the time needed to write a novel militates against them ever getting written. Certain established, successful writers will claim that those who desire to write *will* write and any excuse is merely an excuse for the inability to write. It is hard to believe that these people have ever experienced directly the countless pressures and demands which hamper thought, let alone writing, that are the everyday circumstances of most of the people connected to Federation groups. Tillie Olsen, the American writer, is eloquent upon this subject:

How much it takes to become a writer. Bent (far more common than we assume), circumstances, time, development of craft – but beyond that: How much conviction as to the importance of what one has to say, one's right to say it. And the will, the measureless store of belief in oneself to be able to come to, cleave to, find the form for one's own life comprehensions. Difficult for any male not born into a class that breeds such confidence. Almost impossible for a girl, a woman.   —*Silences p.256*

We have to recognise the sheer difficulty of sustaining a long fiction in brief snatches of writing time. Material conditions profoundly affect the forms which people choose to express their experiences. However, considerations of such mundane matters as money, space and time rarely appear in literary theory.

This is the reason why so many people write poetry within the Federation – despite poetry being regarded as one of the most mystified and erudite forms of writing within our culture. The great thing about the poem is that it can be short, can be sometimes actually written, revised and finished within the odd quarter of an hour between washing up the Sunday dishes and starting to get tea, or in a spare half hour when the other people in the house are watching television or out at the cinema. The kitchen seems to be the favourite place for writing to many people, both women and men.

Shush — Mum's Writing

Sit down be quiet read a book
Don't you dare to speak or look
Shush Mum's writing

She's left the dishes in the sink
All she does is sit and think
Shush Mum's writing

Nothing for dinner nowt for tea
And all she ever says to me is
Shush Mum's writing

But what's all this Mum's wrote a book
Why not buy one have a look
No need to shush now we can shout
And tell all our friends about
MUM'S WRITING

—*Pat Dallimore*

The short story or 'slice of life' is also a very popular form amongst writers in Federation groups, although it has been a very unpopular form commercially for years. Clearly people are attracted to it because it allows them to get something down in a limited period of time whereas such restrictions would make the writing of a novel an impossible prospect.

Roger Mills wrote *A Comprehensive Education* in a notebook on the tube train journey to and from work; others we know have written poems sitting at the back of Ward Labour Party meetings during procedural discussions, or whilst waiting at the doctor's and so on.

Against all odds, writing *does* happen. In what form does this process of making sense take shape? The first and usual way is often via other forms, not necessarily suited to the experiences which are being represented. Understandably, many writers begin with conventional forms, those which are seen to be literary, what writing should be like. The little tale with a twist in the final sentence is a form which was massively sustained by the Evening Standard Short Story competition. It has always been thought that poetry must rhyme, even at the cost of a truth or an appropriateness. Often poetry is regarded as a device to write about nature, even in places where 'nature' is a rare sight indeed. Romance, expressed as love and emotion by women or action and adventures by men, is frequently adapted to this form. But not all influences from the mainstream or from school are necessarily detrimental. Indeed, the most alive and responsive writing is that which incorporates but transforms elements from literary and/or popular writing. Any attempt to establish rigid, essential forms for working class writing would be doomed to failure.

Poetry in the street

The changes in the mainstream literary world during the 1950's and 60's opened up the possibilities in poetry and are probably largely responsible for the ease in which it is now written. Many people have also been encouraged into writing poetry because of its growing popularity in the culture of rock music – with many groups now paying much more attention to the coherence and originality of the lyrics – even to the extent where many record album covers now print the lyrics as pieces of poetry in their own right. Poets such as Linton Kwesi Johnson and John Cooper-Clarke have attracted an enormous following amongst young people through their association with reggae and punk music. The contribution of these factors has produced a situation whereby writing poetry is no longer such an esoteric activity. It is one of the most available forms and this is reflected in working class writing, where the lyric poem and the combative ballad are well represented. Such democratisation of the form co-exists with the idea that poetry is the most privileged, the most literary of all writing activities. This same sense of poetry as an elite activity is re-inforced at the most symbolic moment of its democratisation: the annual Arts Council sponsored National Poetry Competition. Unlike the very prestigous book awards – the Whitbread, Pullitzer, Booker prizes – in which publishers and/or literary intellectuals submit and then vote on already published work, anyone can enter the National Poetry Competition, provided their poem is within the required length and is accompanied by the fee of, usually, £10. There is normally a phenomenal entry and, just before the prize is awarded to an already established, published poet, one of the judges is almost bound to comment in tones of polite outrage that 'anyone thinks they can write a poem'.

Writing is about the adaptation of old forms to create new forms or to serve new purposes within representation. One of the most successful ways in which this has happened is in the move away from poetry as something which is read, privately and silently, to poetry as performance shading into cabaret and drama. It is difficult to write about that process except to say that it happens and that the power and the excitement is as much in the audience as in the performance. Poetry readings, as we've seen earlier, are a very important part of the new social relations being forged around writing. The effect of this on the forms of writing is, simply, that they are often written to be spoken as well as, or instead of, to be read to oneself. This has effects on the rhythms of the writing, particularly as it is often a rhythm of speech with dialect inflections. The staging of a poetry reading or of a performance often leads groups to isolate out and concentrate on the dramatic. In some areas, Liverpool for example, there is a real commitment to the production of plays. In Liverpool this has been helped by the playwriting course run by the University Extension in which potential playwrights work with established authors in the context of real plays, real stages and real performances. Elsewhere, London and Manchester particularly, the growth of new wave cabaret, where songs, satire, sketches and stand up comic routines have been revived, has provided a new outlet and a new challenge to some working class writers.

The autobiographical tradition

The use of the autobiographical mode has recently generated strenuous debate. Much of the power of the autobiography, as a literary form which is linked to traditions of political resistance, comes from its contrast to the conventions of standard biography. In the hands of working class writers this power comes from its distance from the usual subjects of autobiography. Biographies are usually written about the rich and powerful, they register the worth of an individual's life as well as conferring a sense of importance. The usual authors of autobiographies, often ghost written, are politicians, film and media stars – as in biography, people who are prominent in public life. But the autobiographical form also has a history which links it to working class experience and to political struggle.

Since the 17th century, some non-conformist traditions have encouraged the personal testimony as a prelude to the act of conversion. Individuals were encouraged to describe their past lives at length, their errors and trials, to confess to their previous histories before starting their second life as one of the saved. The tradition also has more directly political antecedents. In many state trials in the 19th century, the usual defence of working class political activists standing trial for illegal or insurrectionary politics was a statement of the harshness and misery of the life that had brought them inescapably to political action. These can be studied in Patricia Hollis's book *Class and Class Conflict in 19th Century England* from which Richard Pilling's defence, for example, is taken:

Gentlemen, I am somewhere about 43 years of age. I was asked last night if I were not 60. But if I had as good usage as others, instead of looking like a man of 60, I should look something like a man of 35... (here follow pages of personal testimony concerning the growth of political awareness)... And now, gentlemen of the jury, you have the case before you; the masters conspired to kill me, and I combined to keep myself alive.

This kind of connection between the political and the deeply personal can also be seen in contemporary autobiography. Sabir Sandali's deeply moving autobiography, *Small Accidents,* written whilst still at school, about his experience as a young Asian in Uganda before his family fled to England, ends with his own reflection on the moment of writing his account.

It's eight o'clock on a typical November evening. I can hear the cars swishing away along the wet roads. It's exactly twenty-one months since my father died. Nothing seems to be happening. My brothers and sisters are downstairs, glued to the television, and here I am, sitting at a table, thinking and scribbling down memories, wondering whether I'll ever be able to remember my past, when I was a young kid of nine, being entered into public school for the first time – the days when I didn't have much to worry about. I remember playing marbles in the sand behind our house. I'm crowded by my friends, excited because I've won.

I remember the epic journey to my secondary school. Be it cold, windy, rainy or sunny, I get my bike ready to start, to once again ride wildly through the fog patch – and then I remember the black, tortured man, hands cut off, the smell of kerosene polluting the fresh morning atmosphere...

Here, as in much Federation writing, the purpose of such writing is a making sense: not a making beautiful or making entertainment but a making of sense for the self and for others. Some autobiographical writing has had very direct results:

Last week I was sent a copy of the Leeds bulletin 'TUCRIC' (Trades Union & Community Resource Information Centre) which contained a review of my book, a review which gave me great pleasure because the reviewer, evidently a factory worker, said he had started reading it when feeling very depressed, because at the time the workers in his factory were faced with a situation affecting their wages and conditions which he thought they couldn't win. After reading the book he was so stimulated that he was able to think out a new strategy which brought victory for himself and fellow-workers. It had made every minute that I had spent writing the book worthwhile, even if it was only for that one instance.   —Ernie Benson, author of '*To Struggle is to Live*', in a letter to another writer

Some people have written their autobiographies quite independently of any local publishing initiative, often not with a view to publication but simply to get down on paper a record of what their lives had been like. Ron Barnes' first book, *A Licence to Live,* was written to be passed on to his daughter. Ernie Benson wrote *To Struggle is to Live* after a number of people had asked him 'Why don't you put it in writing?', after hearing his various anecdotes. Federation groups continue to receive unsolicited autobiographies from people throughout the country who have come across their names and who seek an opinion on the suitability of publication for their work. Unfortunately, not all of these requests can be followed up because the writer lives beyond the publishing constituency of the group. Other people have been prompted to write because of some personal crisis or change of circumstances often linked to love, death or illness. Martha Lang wrote *An Austrian Cockney* during the time she had left over while looking after her invalid husband. Leslie Wilson's *Dobroyed* was written in diaries during a stay at an approved school and then re-worked afterwards into its final form.

And then many others have been encouraged to write about their lives by the local publishing initiative themselves. In most cases this has been as a result of a person's reminiscences being taped and then transcribed. This is then made the basis for subsequent revision, addition, joint or collective editorial working, so that the end product is not simply a transcript but a piece of writing that has developed out of the spoken word. The directness of speech often gives particular strength and accessibility to these books.

Many of the books published by Federation groups were produced in this way, often by literacy students in co-operation with teachers and other students. So, personal experience, the autobiographical, dominates local publishing activity. Its expression, though, is not just through direct autobiography but also poems and short stories.

The most usual way in which people represent their experience is currently through 'realism', though with recent moves towards playwriting and mixed media productions (e.g. music and words) this may well be changing. 'Realism' is a loaded term, carrying with it a number of pejorative connotations. For many 'realism' means something unattractive because it is equated with 'kitchen sink drama', with 'downers', bleak pessimism and squalor.

But people who have expressed reservations about 'books which just tell you how bad everything used to be and still is' are often surprised to find that realism can also be about inspiring feats of personal heroism in the face of dreadful handicaps. That it gives an account of much selflesness amongst many people in life, that it is often covering periods of great reflective happiness and is an appreciation of the minutiae of everyday experience. And when they are read, as they have been in their hundreds of thousands, many people are highly appreciative of the fact that for once common experience is given the dignity and significance which it deserves. Through such books many people are able to find large parts of themselves because they shared the same or a similar environment or experiences.

The detailed autobiography can also function as a 'general autobiography' – one that reflects, details, analyses and critically validates much of what has been lived in common with others.

There has been criticism recently of such local autobiographies by socialists who feel that individual accounts of personal experiences are so subjective and localised that they may in fact militate against a collective, socialist project by confirming the individualism of social experience so central to capitalist and puritan ideology.

The clearest example of this approach is perhaps that adopted by Chris Miller in his review of *QueenSpark* in the *Head and Hand* review of books:

They do not attempt to produce a socialist understanding of their history, and are much more likely to talk about 'working people' rather than 'working class'... one doesn't 'make history' through the writing of autobiographies... consequently they are unable to confront what are basically reactionary ideas. They are silent when a writer's understanding is simply a reflection of bourgeois thinking, and fall into the trap that because it's from the working class then it must be good.

Where such criticism fails for us is in the assumption that everybody knows exactly what socialism is, knows that they want it and knows how to get it. Working people do not cease to be the bundle of contradictory, often bourgeois ideas and feelings, when you start calling them a class and not a people. Of course it is easier to publish only the autobiographies of militant shop stewards to propogate the myth that this represents the truly authentic working class experience. But then that leaves the majority of working people behind with nothing of any value to contribute to the making of socialism, wherever she may take us.

To raise these issues of writing, culture and politics is, evidently, to open a Pandora's box of problems. But it seems unavoidable that we should open that box — having done so we then need to take a look inside.

The cultural minefield

Every discussion on culture that took place among the group involved in this book led us into a minefield. When it came to 'middle-class culture', 'working-class culture', then to the 'State', 'hegemony', 'dominant and subordinate', then on to bar billiards, the relationship between our bank managers and the bourgeois literary tradition... well, the mines began to go off.

But we could not get away from it. Early in our collective work we each went away and wrote a separate paper on what we understood by 'working class culture'. These we found individually helpful and they were also necessary in order to try to clear our heads. But while these papers were useful to us and helped to clarify certain points they still did not feed directly into the text of the book. When it came to the final draft, the person who offered the penultimate text on 'Working Class Culture — What does it mean?' got more flack from the rest of us than any of the other writers who wrote sections for this book. We found it extraordinarily difficult to agree on a consecutive flow of argument: difficult, too, to disagree constructively on the text offered in a way that would fundamentally improve it. Yet we were a group with deep basic agreements, with a lot of shared cultural and political practice.

We were convinced, however, that the problems which 'culture/ working-class culture' etc, pointed to were not trivial. We felt that the academic language in which these issues have generally been debated might baffle and annoy many of the people whose work this book is about. But we also felt that the issues, in themselves, were important enough for us to have to try to clarify them. They are issues which have a real bearing on how we communicate with each other.

We came to the conclusion that we couldn't even in the most general sense, get it right. This was not due to any lack of time, or goodwill. It was the very importance of the topic, the words and phrases themselves as labels for central areas of class conflict, that caused us to go round and round the subject. It would have been easy to be 'objectively correct', to have held all our terms constant, other things equal, fact apart from value. We could perhaps have got our definitions 'right', but only at the cost of getting everything else wrong. It is all too easy to end up as world champion of a game which only you and your six best friends can play. To be abstract in this area seemed to do violence to what many of us thought of as complex realities. In the end, we did not want to run away with a smoothing iron and flatten our arguments.

Instead we present them as assertions and questions, finished and unfinished propositions.

☐ Working class and popular culture is not necessarily anti-capitalist. There'll be no prize for mole catchers waiting for the class to surface one day unsullied by capitalism. Such expectations are as unrealistic as the view that produces a nostalgic and pure picture of the working class, a dominated but heroically untainted force. FWWCP books and groups are not really into that kind of super-heroics. Indeed we have produced a lot of material, much to the irritation of some socialists, which makes a nonsense of it.

☐ Established cultural institutions are not simply one-way conveyor belts for ruling class ideology: nor are working class people and communities blank slates upon which those cultural institutions can, at will, write. Cultural relations are matters of negotiation, contest, struggle. The frontiers shift, bits are bought, incorporated and changed by both sides in the struggle.

☐ What is special about cultural struggle is that it is never safe from a ruling class point of view. Communication is never 100% safe even when the communicators have very advanced technologies, know exactly what they wish to communicate *and* have a tradition-less, supine audience upon which to play. Hands up those who are signed-up members of the 'masses'! While rulers can successfully, to an extent, use cultural weapons as instruments of domination, to that same extent they must engage themselves with *some* of the real needs, desires and capacities of the oppressed in such a way as to make it possible to swing the sword back the other way.

☐ There *is* some space to work in culturally towards better relations of production and a different society from the one we have now. And rather *now* than 'after the revolution'. But that space cannot be occupied without interference from outside. It cannot be used effectively for the project of cultural liberation without using many of the forms, technologies, ideas and, yes, even the 'values' used outside. To allow the 'middle-class' to enclose and exclusively possess values which they profess to adhere to like democracy, art, culture... to let them call such things 'middle-class' and then to allow *ourselves* to give these things up by calling them 'bourgeois democracy' etc, is to give far too much away and thus to continue to remain ineffectively isolated.

It ain't what you do, it's the way that you do it...

Of course, there are differences and bitter conflicts in the cultural field, apart from those over wages or party labels, between working people and the bourgeoisie. But workers have always adapted, and used for their own purposes, literary and other forms designed by others for other purposes. This is a strength, not a weakness. 'Consumers' also use and enjoy products in many ways quite foreign to their makers and promoters. There are some areas (meanings and signs are among them) which can never be closed and which historically oppressed people have been amazingly inventive in keeping open.

Much of what we regard in retrospect as working class culture was based on the adaptation of existing bourgeois forms. This is certainly true in the literary field where Chartist writers adopted the novel for their own purposes − a classic literary form − as well as using elaborate verse forms which they had come to know through their reading of established poets like Shelley, Milton and Byron. The many 'Handel' societies which flourished in working class communities in the late 19th century, committed to an annual production of 'The Messiah', represented an absorption by many working class people of something from the bourgeois cultural tradition which they particularly wanted. The many choirs and bands associated with specific pits or industrial workplaces should not be defined culturally by the music they played − which was often classical, court and palace in origin − but by the way it was performed within a completely different set of social relationships, which gave the music a quite different social meaning from that intended by its composers.

When we look to the power of the State and its Health Service, Arts Councils etc, we can see them as contested public areas, sites of struggle through which we can push for reforms, defences and partial victories. Of course, the dice are loaded in this game. It will be the dominant groups who will determine the form in which the demands — for trade union rights, for education or health care — are to be met. Yes, you can have trade unions, an education system, a health service but these must take certain regulated forms. The power to define and control the form in which these demands are to be met is central — but that does not mean that the contradictions then disappear or that the systems of control work smoothly and without opposition.

The culture industry:
tensions and contradictions

We may find life contradictory, but so do capitalists. They compete with each other, and are not a single united force. Spaces for struggle and subversion do exist. Here we need to be aware of the contradiction between the interests of the individual capitalist to make the maximum profit for himself by producing any commodity, no matter how subversive, for which there is effective demand, and the interests of the capitalist class as a whole to secure the social foundations of capitalism against subversion. Hence the need for state intervention, monopolies commissions, obscenity laws and so on, as part of the attempt to 'police' these contradictions.

Many people on the left talk about 'the media' and the entertainment industry, as if they were highly effective machines driven by their Capitalist Drivers simply to inject 'bourgeois ideology' (or some such Bad Thing) directly into the heads of their (presumably passive and gullible) audience. But people do not read novels or go to movies in order to consume bourgeois ideology. These commodities are consumed because the individuals concerned think that they will derive pleasure, in some form, from their consumption. Now, it may be that they will be exposed to ideology in the process of getting that pleasure — but who's to say that an audience necessarily takes a programme or a film the way it was intended? What the different people who make up the audience for the TV news get out of it on any given night is likely to be quite different from what the journalists and newscasters thought they were putting into it. Consumers of all kinds of cultural commodities frequently find uses for those commodities which are quite different from those which their makers intended. Those who took the white man's Bible to Africa to civilise the natives could never have foreseen the ways in which black people have taken those biblical stories of oppression and exile and transformed their meaning — so that 'Babylon' now refers to the homelands of those who exported the Bible.

In the world of commercial culture profits may get made. But a whole lot of other cultural processes (not all of them necessarily in tune with the interests of the profiteers) may go on at the same time. This is to say the relation of commercial culture to working class culture is a contradictory and unstable thing, a process of consumption, but also of subversion and transformation — not a process in which a 'dominant ideology' is simply imposed, from the outside, on the working class.

Relations of commercial exploitation also involve, simultaneously, the begging, borrowing and modification of different modes of cultural expression. Sometimes this takes the form of hacking out spaces in which to breathe within dominant institutions, sometimes building alternatives, sometimes taking the micky out of prescribed forms. There's a whole tradition of socialist songs based on the principle of parodying the dominant forms so that they are, as it were, made to speak of their own contradictions — most well known perhaps is Joe Hill's rewrite of a Salvation Army song to produce 'You'll get Pie in The Sky When You Die'. More materially, the 'work to rule' is the most obvious example of the way in which an oppressive system can be made to run in reverse, or to grind to a halt.

Working class cultures

Any notion of working class culture as a thing apart, in its own space, needing to be defended and kept pure from the encroachments of the media is misleading. It just doesn't seem to be useful to think of different cultures (commercial culture, working class culture) as if they occupied distinct and different social spaces. Cultures have to be seen as embedded in contradictory ways in the same spaces or institutions. This also means that, rather than thinking of some simple opposition — a unified Them versus a unified Us, it may be more useful to think in plurals. We need to think of working class culture not as some unified and monolithic thing, but of the many different varieties and forms of working class culture — the cultures of feminity and masculinity, of work, of youth, of the street, of locality, in short of the many different subcultures that exist within the class.

By posing the question in terms of something called middle class culture, as opposed to something called working class culture, we may be getting off on the wrong foot, by assuming that a class to be worthy of the name, must possess a unified homogeneous culture all of its own. But once we accept that the historical and contemporary experience of different groups within the working class has been immensely varied, we should not be surprised that the cultural forms of expression of those experiences are varied too. There is no one unified working class culture, but rather a plurality of forms – as different as those of bowls, reggae and dressmaking.

Similarly, we would like to resist the familiar but simplistic equations that common sense makes between economic categories and cultural traditions. People often speak of middle class culture as if to suggest that bank managers and civil servants, for example, are the natural inheritors of all that is best in the European artistic traditions – as if these people spent their evenings discussing impressionist painting while listening to Chopin.

We cannot assume the existence of some common working class experience and culture – a person is never simply a member of the working class, but always also a member of a particular gender, a particular race, living in a particular locality, etc. These other factors have to be seen as producing important differences in the experience of people who may all be working class in the economic sense, but whose varied experiences are expressed in a range of different cultural forms.

It has to be admitted that working class culture has often been defined in terms of male activity, with the interests of women being of secondary importance. Much contemporary writing by working class people, particularly women, centres on recalling and describing such inequalities and looks forward to ways of breaking down the rigid sex-roles which have been inherited from past social relationships. It also has to be acknowledged that British working class traditions were formed in the midst of one of the most powerful imperialist empires historically known, and even today colonialist and racialist sentiments are still widely expressed amongst working class people as much as in other sectors of the society (see Jeremy Seabrook's book *'What Went Wrong?'*, Gollancz, 1978 for more on this).

It is also true that generational conflicts within working class communities are often as powerful as class conflicts. A number of young working class writers have expressed the feeling that their strongest sense of alienation was first felt as an alienation from what they perceived as adult society in general, and this provided them with the anger which they transformed into various kinds of written and spoken expression. In many cases involvement in writers' workshops and local history projects has brought the different generations much closer together in the process of sharing experiences. But, at times, local history projects which have attempted to portray whole communities – *Changing Times* in a Durham pit village, *The Island* in an East London neighbourhood – have disc!osed a rupture in the continuity of working class life between the generations. Huw Beynon, in a review of the Centerprise publications referring specifically to the debate about generational differences sparked off by the publication of *Strong Words,* has this to say:

A dialogue started, and at one point a young lad said, 'We can see from the way you older ones talk about your lives that you had something to be proud of. But what have us younger ones got to be proud of? We've got nothing like that'.

In *Working Lives,* Ken Jacobs, a Hackney postman, put it another way:

You hear a lot of stories about the old post office... but you take that with a pinch of salt... The kinds of jobs have altered but so have the way in which they related to other aspects of life.

Localities and communities

It's often assumed that the essence of working class culture is to be found in a set of concerns with locality and with forms of solidarity built up around the labour and trade union movements. The problem is these cultural forms grew up in particular historical circumstances. As these circumstances change, the same cultural forms and institutions take on new and different meanings. Firstly, in the context of post war patterns of migration and settlement, the notion of working class culture being based on the defence of a particular cultural identity in a given locality can easily slip over into reactionary forms of parochialism and racism. We have to recognise, for instance, that a traditional site of working class solidarity and good humour, such as the Saturday afternoon football crowd, can and in some cases has become a site for the development of the narrowest forms of intolerant racism and machismo.

The organisational forms of the labour and trade union movements grew up around the institution of labour in the factory. But, as economic circumstances change, in the inner cities, factories are being closed down and production is reorganised on outwork principles. In these circumstances, the organisational forms of solidarity and resistance have to change as well. It will not do to elevate one particular historical form of working class culture and organisation to a point where it is seen as the fixed standard, the essence of what working class culture has to be.

One important question for us is that of when, and in what circumstances, do working class people consciously try to 'make culture'? What for, in what forms, and why is writing currently among them? If we approach the question of working class culture this way, then one of the things that becomes immediately apparent is that it's particular groups, affected by determinants beyond those simply of class, who are most evident among those consciously 'making culture' in the form of writing. Here we mean, for example, people for whom the momentum of their material lives has been severely dislocated – by structural economic changes (Scotland Road and Liverpool 8; Strong Words in the North East); old people in traditional industrial communities threatened by change (East Bowling in Bradford; the People's Autobiography Group in Hackney); migrants who have to redefine themselves in a new life (the Gatehouse project in Manchester; Black Ink in Brixton); women trying to redefine themselves through new forms of consciousness (the Women and Words group in Birmingham: the group from Knowle West estate in Bristol who produced *Shush Mum's Writing*); people uprooted within the country (the Partington Lifetimes project); young people facing possibly permanent unemployment (Fred's People: Our Streets Our Lives from Newcastle). From the variety of circumstances in which these different groups are operating it follows that the cultural forms through which they express their experiences are very different – and these forms cannot be understood simply in relation to class structures – they have to be understood in their relations to patriarchy, imperialism and racism.

Language and culture: bricks and mortar

So far we've talked about culture – but the principal mode through which culture is expressed is that of language. If we live in the house of culture, then it's built with the bricks and mortar of language. Similarly, we cannot talk about literature without talking about literacy – indeed the separation of these two terms is a very recent historical phenomenon, even if it is a separation we tend to take for granted. To remake these connections is one way to begin to be able to speak about the ways in which literature, (built as it is out of language used in certain particular styles and manners) has been 'elevated' to a position where it is often difficult for working class people to break into the circuit of its meanings.

Language has been for many centuries one of the main forms in which class and cultural differences have been expressed. But these differences inevitably express power relations as well. Language can't be seen merely as a neutral instrument which we all use for the purpose of communication – language is intimately bound up with social power and prestige. So deep are the prejudices about certain kinds of speech in our society that language, and especially speech, is always a contentious issue and at times an explosive one. Certainly it is an area that is carefully 'policed' in the key institutions of cultural transmission – until recently the BBC had someone with the Orwellian title of 'Director of the Spoken Word'.

Indeed, these issues are by no means dead and buried. As recently as March 1981 the BBC prepared a 'guide' for announcers and presenters on their radio networks 'The Spoken Word: A Guide to Preferred Usage', written for them by the chief editor of the Oxford English Dictionaries. The Guide was designed to direct BBC personnel towards 'the best... of educated English, in its standard form'. Indeed, the point is clear:

The form of speech recommended is that of a person brought up in one of the Home Counties, educated at one of the established southern universities, for example, Oxford or Cambridge...

The proper way to talk

Speech is intimately connected with locality and class; dialect comes through locality, speech style is inherited through the family and within the neighbourhood peer group, and therefore through class. Speech locates us within the social structure of British society more immediately than any other kind of personal and social characteristic which we may possess. Powerful evaluative processes are continually at work elevating some registers of speech and subordinating others.

As Raymond Williams has pointed out (in his essay on speech in *The Long Revolution*): 'We can trace the minor relics of class prejudice in the lasting equation of moral qualities with class names – base, villain, boor and churl for the poor; kind, free, gentle, noble for the rich'. These connotations have lasted for 600 years. During that time, a particular definition of 'Standard English' has been developed – a particular definition of the Correct Form of the language, which offers itself, commonsensically, as natural, timeless and inevitable. Now, of course, this Standard can be adapted to meet changing times and circumstances – new words are admitted to the Oxford dictionaries, and the media, in their contemporary 'populist' phrase, are less insistent on a Home Counties Standard English form of speaking than they used to be. However, these are marginal adjustments to a system which is premised on the massive metropolitan dominance of that form of the language that happened to grow up in that part of the country where the court and the early universities happened to be established. This then is a crucial dimension of oppression, through which the Correct Form of the language, directly tied in to the structures of economic and political power in the society, becomes an oppressive standard against which all other regional forms and dialects are judged incorrect or inferior – or, at best, are tolerated as 'quaint'.

This is where language is connected to power relations – in terms of the social processes through which one way of speaking comes to be defined as correct and others as incorrent, and in terms of the social processes through which speakers of non-standard forms of the language are encouraged to internalise a sense of their inferiority.

However, just as there are a number of dimensions of oppression, there are a number of forms of resistance, none of them immediately reducible to the outlines of the class system alone. We live in a society in which different groups (and the same people at different times) are subordinate by virtue of their class, race, gender, age or geographical position. Patriarchy, imperialism and racism come to bear on language as they do on culture – indeed they are embedded in the basic structures of our language. Dale Spender amongst others has argued (in her book *Man Made Language* Routledge & Kegan Paul, 1981) that many aspects of the language we speak, right down to the equation of 'people' with men in the use of the pronoun 'he' when gender is unspecified, are structured along the lines of gender, and that this gives rise to a whole set of particular difficulties for women speaking and writing.

Our language is also structured by a set of racist concepts and categories, right the way down from the equations between black and evil, and between white and purity which stand at the centre of the culture. This is linked to the way in which the destruction of forms of Black English (eg the standard double negative in W. Indian English being outlawed as 'wrong') is more violent and more systematic than the similar destruction of forms of non-standard English among the white working class. This is so to such an extent that these standards are often internalised by the members of the oppressed groups (so that they come to regard themselves as in some way linguistically inferior). Then again, some black activists argue that it is important for black people to be able to speak the standard forms of the language if they are not to be consigned to the ghetto of educational failure by virtue of their 'failure' to master the correct standard.

More sharply, Franz Fanon argues that the first impulse of the black man is 'to say no to all those who attempt to build a definition of him'. Jean Genet, in his introduction to George Jackson's *Prison*

Letters, takes the point further. He suggests that black writers, striving to express themselves in 'the language of the master' are caught in a double blind. As Genet puts it 'It is perhaps a new source of anguish for the black man to realise that if he writes a masterpiece it is in his enemy's language, it is his enemy's treasury which is enriched by the additional jewel he has carved' — his only option then is to 'accept this language, but to corrupt it so skilfully that the white men are caught in his trap'.

Since compulsory education began in Britain in the 1870's the majority of school children have been criticised for the language that they have been brought up to use at home, and offered an alternative to admire and emulate based on the 'Received Standard' — nowadays expressed in the speech of the BBC news-reader.

This perspective has dominated the teaching of English in schools for some fifty years — at least since the publication of the Newbolt Report in 1921. The strength of the condemnation of working class speech inherent in this perspective deserves to be seen at some length.

Speech training must be undertaken from the outset... Teachers of infants sometimes complain that when the children come to school they can scarcely speak at all. They should regard this rather as an advantage... It is emphatically the business of the elementary school to teach all its pupils who either speak a definite dialect or whose speech is disfigured by vulgarisms, to speak standard English, and to speak it clearly... The great difficulty of teachers in elementary schools in many districts is that they have to fight against the powerful influence of evil habits of speech contracted in home and street. The teacher's struggle is thus not with ignorance but with a perverted power...

—*Extract from the 'Newbolt Report on English Teaching'.*

The report dates from 50 years ago, as we've said but, unfortunately, this is a perspective on language which still holds in many schools.

Internalising inferiority

So intensively has this idea of linguistic inferiority been promoted that even today, some millions of people continue to feel embarrassed about their own style of speech when put in contexts outside the familiar world of work and neighbourhood.

One of the main areas of difficulty we meet in Britain is the very complex area of pressure, restraint, anxiety around the different modes of speech which are class linked and which — where there's a whole set of cross-pressures between class and region...

... I was asked, it must be now 20 years ago, by a group of active trade unionists to run a class for them on public speaking — elocution — it would have been. And er precisely because these were men er with natural — accustomed to taking a social lead, they were actually most of them very fluent men, very intelligent men, but in this very particular complex of British culture with those cross pressures, they had certain worries which you couldn't argue them out of theoretically. You know — er — about what are called mistakes in grammar, about pronunciation as it's said.

—*Raymond Williams in discussion at a CNAA conference on Communication Studies, 28.11.73.*

Speakers of regional or class dialects are still laughed at, ridiculed or mimicked for their speech, or alternatively have to adopt a hybrid and stilted 'proper' voice when being interviewed on the radio or television, because of the deep snobbery within the mass media with regard to anything other than 'Standard English'. Yet, despite centuries of ridicule and ostracism, it is significant how deeply class and regional accents resist incorporation and are handed on:

TO GET TO THE TOP,
TALK PROPER *by Bryan Silcock*

A person with a 'Standard English' accent is rated as more intelligent than one with a regional accent by sixth-form children and they respond more to him, according to Dr Howard Giles of University College...

Carol Browne is a teacher herself now, but when she arrived from St Kitts her first teachers mistook her dialect hang-ups for stupidity.

—*Observer Magazine, 16 December 1973.*

The same words but different meanings...

When a particular group of people say 'house', 'home', 'dinner', 'tea' or 'supper' the general term contains a specific sense: Homes/ houses of a particular kind, dinners, teas, suppers at certain times of day and with expected sorts of food and drink. These general terms, in other words, involve specific expectations. To put it another way, the general terms derive their meanings from the social contexts in which they are used; this is how people of the same group understand one another and why outsiders often find it difficult. Standard (or 'official') English language and thought does not stand in an abstract relation to these particular contexts though it is claimed that the standard language represents some 'general' interest. In fact the standard language represents a group for whom just such small words like 'house' or 'tea' do have a quite specific content — located in the social backgrounds of a particular section of the society.

Within a working class group (although there will be differences across the counties of the United Kingdom here) we understand what it means to be invited to tea in someone's home. We also would know to expect something different if invited to take tea in, say, the Queen's home or at 10 Downing Street. There is also, quite literally, a world of difference between 'come round for supper' and 'come round for some dinner'. But these simple terms like 'home' and 'tea' also have different meanings *within* the group. Between genders, for example, and between age groups, 'having dinner' means different kinds of task, work, responsibility and commitment/worry.

Now when different groups use what seem the same terms they think and mean differently with them. They also, of course, use different terms — what we have been taught to think of as dialect words or phrases. The complex that we refer to as culture is quite literally all those different systems of thought and expression, intention and understanding. Popular television serials and series recognise this and know they have to 'get it right' for their working class audiences — they still, of course, very often get it wrong. Popular personalities (like Radio 1 DJ's) and politicians also trade on this use of working class terms and figures of speech, but they too get it wrong — like Harold Wilson's statement about people putting their bills under (instead of behind) the clock or ornaments on the mantlepiece, or Tony Blackburn speaking about men going to work with their sandwiches wrapped in newspaper.

These different systems of understanding the world are not abstract; they are as real and material as the differences they represent. The so-called proper speech of the BBC and the proper writing of school textbooks, official forms, scientific explanations and, above all, the Law, all these operate to make us feel stupid, outside what is acceptable, old-fashioned and not quite all there. In this way they continue what most of us felt and cried over at school — 'the hard red cross of intelligence' one poet called it, and the instruction to 'do it again, properly'.

'Getting on' at school and society involves paying a very high price, the suppressing of what we feel to be parts of our identity, in favour of writing and speaking and thinking in ways that we may feel are uncomfortable and strange. Thomas Carlyle explained this by a useful analogy, he spoke about language as being like clothing. We often feel the language we have to use does not quite 'fit the facts', does not enable us to feel properly or fully, hems us in, seems to pinch or sag here and there, restricts our movement and so on. The most dramatic example of this is being in a courtroom as a witness or, alas, in the dock! We feel out of place, foolish, not in control. But this is really only the extreme example of how all forms of organised communication minimises what is distinctive about different groups in favour of some general bland language that expresses only the expectations and needs of the middle classes. Again gender experiences cut across all of this, as do age, ethnic, regional and national differences.

So, to sum up, this distinction between a way of life, thought and language that 'fits' and the many that do not, penetrates our inner-most sense of ourselves and makes it difficult to express what we feel and experience. Given, as we have discussed already, the domin-ation in our society of the means of expression and communication by particular groups, it is little wonder that most people live in semi-silence until, as Thomas Carlyle also said, their actions speak out loud, in a language most strange. Although there have always been rich and poor (so we are told on good authority), and men have always been the masters of their own houses, these forms of domination – like the conquest of one nation by another – differ under capitalism from earlier times. We think one particular feature of this difference is the domination of the means of expression, including the attempt to deny different groups their own voice and ways of thought. That is why initiatives by ordinary women and men through organisations like the Federation are actually far more important than even their very significant sales and organisational consequences.

Repairing the damage

As far as all this contributes to what writers and groups in working-class neighbourhoods do, it gives them a double task: to repair damage, and to develop a self-assertive fight back. Many people are convinced that the language they use just won't do for purposes of thought and creation, or indeed for anything on paper. For some this amounts to an inhibition from writing so great that it can only be got over by tape and transcript, or by having their words taken down for them by a listener who believes in their validity. For others, what they are led to produce is the kind of stilted language that comes from dressing up your meaning in a form that you may not practise enough for it to come easily, or that you may not have the confi-dence to criticise or vary. Federation books aren't free of this kind of stiffness. But freeing writers from these anxieties is an aim both of the direct encounters in groups, and of the growing body of published work.

Where the writers do think and create in the common tongues, it's worth looking at some instances where the work's statement includes a statement about language, either made in so many words or by the writer's working choices. There is dialect writing as such; few people now exploit it across a wide range of tones and subjects, but there is Fred Reed's *Cumen and Gannin,* in which he has chosen to use spelling imitative of the spoken sounds of Northumbrian dialect over a range of satirical, lyric and contemplative verse.

Seedin

Whaat ends wi' borth and whaat begins wi' endin?
Dust t' dust or life t' life ascendin?
Wheor mild coos meditate betwixt theor feedin
A women wi' a scythe lops thistles seedin.
She's not alen. A bairn is in hor womb
That tiv hor lusty sweepins will succomb.

There are many more people who less self-consciously maintain the rhythms and turns of thought and expression of a region, most easily identifiable through local uses and slangs but going beyond that. This is all London:

Now why he always worked at night was that it was easier to rook a half-drunk toff at night coming out of the night clubs, than what it was to rook somebody in the daytime, that just wanted a station job done.
— *Lil Smith, 'The Good Old Bad Old Days', Centerprise.*

– just as this is all Yorkshire:

My memories of Bowling Tide are mostly of hard work with as much fun pushed in as possible. I worked in Harold Mills' cobblers' hut just on one side of the Tide Field and we were always overfaced with work during Bowling Tide week. With it being holiday week, we'd plenty of working boots to mend and when the Tidefolk came they fetched all theirs as well. They used to save them while they came to Bowling.
— *'Bowling Tidings', East Bowling History Workshop.*

Writers also reflect on local usages, as Jim Wolveridge does in *Ain't it Grand?* and *The Muvver Tongue,* or as an incidental but essential part of explaining a condition of life, like Terence Monaghan in *Hello, are you working?*

You grew up with this complex. You were afraid of things. You were nulled.

It means that you were afraid. There's more to it than just being afraid. You were humbled, cowed. There's a tremendous lot of descriptions you can apply to the word 'nulled'. You were nulled because of circumstances. Because of life.

Some writers make the judgement — important in the light of discussions of the range and kind of thought and generalisation that particular forms of language can carry — that standard English is appropriate for narrative, and the local lingo for dialogue. A.S. Jasper wrote *A Hoxton Childhood* this way, about his childhood before the first world war; and a recent and interesting example is Errol O'Connor's *Jamaica Child* — interesting because part of what it is about is the existence of a culture of riddles, old stories and traditions, and the mixture of warmth and scepticism with which it is received:

I asked Papa why the sun shone in the daytime and the moon at night. He explained it to me, but I never did understand what he was talking about. After some time explaining, somehow he saw the dumb look on my face. So he explained it another way, the way I liked best.

Millions an' millions of 'ears ago, when only de moon an' de sun was about, Papa began, de sun an' de moon use to shine in de daytime togeda, because dey was good, good fren' den. Time go by an' de moon became grumbly an' neva satisfied... anyway, de sun try an' try fe pleas de greedy moon, but de moon still neva satisfi. So one deay de sun start fe quarril wid de moon. Soon dey was fighting...

These writers may be partly concerned to demonstrate that they can use standard language with skill. Toby, the tramp in Bristol Broadsides' book, goes further; he has learned to reproduce the use of high-falutin language to bamboozle and assert power, usually in situations when he is fighting up from under:

The Social Security once suggested to me that I go to Winterbourne Rehabilitation Centre. I said, Gentlemen, I have neither the desire nor inclination to form an alliance with such an establishment, with its misfits who have taken a retrograde step into the morass of moral degradation. It would be tantamount to a social indiscretion. A statement like that would leave them somewhat impervious.

The last instance that should be mentioned is Leslie Wilson's *Dobroyed*, a book whose struggle with English spelling was thought by readers and editors to have produced new connections and combinations of ideas. It represented the writer's perceptions too closely to be re-arranged into the standard forms so was published as it was written. This is a sample:

In the afternoon, I took a strong deslike when sitting in a deppresive mood. I watched the time lingger on houre after houre untill I new I was on my last momment and began a comfersation with mother, and the feelling of a strong urge to stay dident help. I new my strong brake of effort had to be made as my time had allready passt the leaving houre, then holiding my smaller brother I kissed him breafly, then put him dawn leaving him with just one or two pats on his head. After whishing mother good-by I was soon enough through the door and can say almost on the verge of kriying as clocing the front door.

This is not a complete catalogue of the relationships between standard and non-standard language that the Federation books demonstrate. Yet it should be enough to make it clear that the writer's relationship with a language which she or he can make free with in more than one form is part of what writing is for, because the exploration of language is partly an exploration of class (or gender or race) position.

This section should also indicate that these books, written as they are by people whose use of English was formed in different places and at different times over 70 or more years, are full of evidence for the debate about language, thought and expression, which we will go on to discuss.

Patterns of language: patterns of thought

There is an intimate connection between the thoughts we think and the words we use. There is also disagreement about what the connection is. Is all thought 'internalised speech', or is it possible to think thoughts without language for them? If not, is language always words? Answers on one side of a postcard only. In any case, it is clear that the range of languages and the range of ideas and beliefs in a particular culture at a particular time, are very closely connected, and that they both differ from those of other cultures and times. Rather than attempting to compare one language with another, we could look at changes in our own, for example, at the developing meanings of words like 'society' and 'moderate'.

The question that arises directly out of this is, are there differences between the range of ideas and beliefs open to people whose thinking has formed in the mould of the different dialects of a language? In other words, if we can say that language use in English relates to class — and we have decided that in spite of the tendency all round to piracy, overlap and perhaps standardisation, we may say this — can we also say that the thoughts we can think relate to class? And if so, would this be a statement about the *restriction* of some thought-and-language forms, or just a statement about different kinds of specialisation?

Educating the educators?

On the basis of this general argument about the close connection between forms of language and forms of thought, it has been argued in recent years (most notably in the massively influential work of the educational sociologist, Basil Bernstein) that the familiarity and closeness of working class communities produces an intimate way of speaking which is quite appropriate and suitable for these contexts, but which is inappropriate and unsuitable for the learning process in school. This argument has then been advanced as one of the main reasons why working class children fail to do well in school – because they are alienated by the formality and abstraction of the language used there. The next step along this argument has been to suggest that there is some kind of structural impasse between the everyday language of working class speech and the rational, intellectual, impersonal languages of scientific, administrative and abstract thought.

Now there is plenty of evidence to support the notion that there is a discontinuity between working class language(s) and the various scientific and theoretical discourses used in the education system. The problem is to explain how that discontinuity comes about. Is it the result of the inherent limitations of working class people, as some right wing educationalists would argue? Or is it the result of the 'cultural deprivation' which working class children are said to suffer in their pre-school years – before they get the benefits of middle class culture and socialisation in school? Or is this discontinuity (the inability of working class children to enter into the formal discourses of the school successfully) simply another word for the prejudices of middle class teachers and administrators – so that children who don't talk like them are seen as linguistically inferior, and children from different backgrounds to their own are seen as 'culturally deprived'?

The discontinuity between working class language(s) and the various scientific and theoretical discourses which are needed to further our understanding of the world we live in may be most directly explained as a result of the ways in which the educational system itself is, and remains, closed to most working class people. If the children are to be designated 'failures' because they can't connect with the language of the school, then the schools ought also to be designated 'failures' if they can't connect with the forms of thought, language and culture which the children bring with them when they arrive at school. But it's not just a question of what happens in school:

I talk as a manual labourer who, at the age of 30, decided that he could benefit more from a university education than employed for life in mass production. I was too tired at the day's end for anything else and I couldn't see the work I was doing leading me anywhere. Many men are similarly placed.

I applied for a place of my choice with 2 good 'A' levels (Grade A and Grade C)...

Everything in the interview seems rigged to undermine the person's confidence. Unless he makes the 'right' impression, that's it. For one particular course I was interviewed by two gentlemen of the Arts faculty...

The tone of the questioning was gossipy and often callous: How come I had so many children? 3 by the age of 30. What age did I start? etc. I was asked about my father's occupation. He is dead but they were interested in what he did. Then the leading interviewer asked me about my last years at school and my early years at work. Leaving no stone unturned he stopped often, queried what I was saying or what I'd written on the form... Then I was asked about 'stamina' in writing essays. Would I be able to keep abreast of the other students? He didn't seem sure. I told him with my experience that would be easy...

They both went outside the room, to discuss something together. When they returned one had to leave and shook my hand, smiling. The other told me, 'I'll have to say No'. Why? My use of English on the form of application and my faulty grammar, when I spoke as well.   —*Extracts from an article on 'Higher Education and the Working Class' by J.A. Jardine in 'W.E.A. News' February 1982.*

Teachers, leaders and theories

Many of these arguments about the inadequacy of everyday speech in coping with abstract thought and theory have not only been advanced by educationalists as explanations of why working class children fail in school, but also by intellectual marxists as explanations of the increasing distrust which many working people have come to feel about abstractions such as 'Socialism' or 'Marxism'. It may be that one part of an explanation of how this distrust has come about might relate to the reluctance of the Labour party, throughout its history, to take any real interest in encouraging political debate and education within the party itself. Evidently, the emphasis on 'cultural politics' in the last few years − out of which this book arises − has been a result of attempts to revive these areas of debate.

But the remaking of a popular socialist culture will not simply happen as a result of people sitting in universities and left publishing houses or socialist conferences producing elegant theories of how and why Capitalism is a Bad Thing. It can't be a question of waiting for the working class (those other people, over there, somewhere) to come and buy the latest Socialist Book and to be converted, with all the religious overtones of that metaphor. Rather, it has to be a question of producing new forms of political practice in daily life which connect with the felt concerns of the majority of people in all areas of life, not just around questions of wages and votes. It's a question of developing new forms of social relationships around the issues that people care deeply about – and of developing a common socialist language out of those day to day practices and relationships. It's no good having brand new Socialist Solutions dreamed up by the vanguard intellectuals to solve everybody else's problems. The very notion of there being one separate category of Thinkers or Theorists (what does that make everybody else!) is part of the problem, and no part of the solution.

Many of the debates that have gone on over the last few years about language and cultural politics have been conducted in an academic context, and in a dense jargon unfamiliar to many people. This in itself may be a good reason for being suspicious of all this 'theory' and for calling for a return of ordinary language and plain speaking. But this might not be much of an answer. For one thing, we can't simply ditch the theory and go back to some unpolluted 'ordinary language' or 'common sense' – at least, not without ending up back inside the terms of the dominant ideologies, and frameworks of thought we want to oppose. Common sense ('A woman's place is in the home') and ordinary language ('queers, wogs, extremists') are heavily colonised by the dominant culture. We certainly need to disentangle 'theory' from its usual equation with a particular and superior category of theorists, teachers and leaders – a category from which most people are, by definition, excluded. But that simply makes theory (or understanding the principles which govern the problem you're facing, whether that's how to build a wall or a sentence) everybody's business, not something we can do without. Just as there is, in our view, no such thing as 'unskilled' labour – for all human labour involves the brain alongside the hand – there can be no knowledge which does not involve some kind of theory, and no political practice which is not based on some theory about, for instance, how power operates. Correspondingly anybody engaged in 'cultural politics' is necessarily working with some set of theories or ideas, implicit or explicit, about how culture operates.

The debate about class and language generated by Bernstein's work is not of merely academic consequence, but directly affects educational policy and day to day teaching in schools. The work of writers such as William Labov and Harold Rosen has been of great value in revealing the depth of social prejudices about the 'proper' way to talk and write, and in revealing the power relations behind the notion that only some groups in the society have what can be called 'culture' (Go to the back of the class all you lot without culture.) Their work is important as part of the struggle to demolish the practices through which everybody other than the speakers of the accepted white middle class forms of language are oppressed and 'failed' in the educational system.

As that critical work has developed, many of Bernstein's theories about the inadequacy of working class language have crumbled in the face of evidence of the strength and subtlety of working class and black languages. A major part of that struggle has been to give speakers of non-standard dialects and languages the support needed if they are not to be made to feel inadequate by the way in which the education system presently defines and processes them as unintelligent, educationally sub-normal, and so on. But we can't be content simply to celebrate the strength and vitality of these ways of speaking. There are problems with the language that any and all of us habitually use, problems which go back to the ways in which our language structures and limits our ways of thinking – sometimes in very negative ways, ways which we often remain unconscious of. The problem here is deep rooted because our ways of thought and speech are habitualised and 'naturalised' as common sense, obvious, beyond question. It's exactly because of this that we need to question our taken-for-granted modes of language – hence the importance of organising debates and developing new practices around the basic issues of language and writing.

It is certainly true that there is much in our existing language which is severely limiting and distorting to the struggle for a different society. We saw earlier in the Raymond Williams quote how class relationships of 600 years ago are still reflected in the value-laden words in use today.

The feminist movement, by the way it struggled with and against sexism in our language, has played a leading role in bringing to attention the deep prejudices and divisive values widespread in everyday language. Women who are 'birds' or 'tarts' are held in as little esteem by the user of such language as the Irishman who is 'Paddy' or 'Mick', the West Indian who is 'Sambo', the Chinese who is a 'Chinky' or the Asian who is a 'Paki'. Language, as a means of definition is also a means of control. Women who refuse to be called 'birds' or 'tarts' or any one of the numerous, belittling and offensive names patriarchy has for them are also refusing the expectations and limitations implied by them. The 'little woman' is standing on her own two, strong feet.

Part of the struggle for different forms of social, economic and cultural relationships involves a linguistic struggle which will *prefigure* the new relationships we seek. And that is why such questions as the words we use when talking to each other and about each other have figured so prominently in the experiences of the individual Federation groups and in the conduct of national Federation business.

One lesson to be drawn from all this is that any one particular form of 'English' will always be partial — however much it may be standardised and institutionalised as the correct form of the language. The argument that certain types of 'non-standard' language are not suitable for use in 'literature' can then be examined in a new light. Language is the very material of literature. If we transpose the arguments about the devaluing of working class experience, and of the forms of language through which that experience is articulated, in the education system, we should perhaps not be surprised if the literary establishment similarly devalues the representation of those experiences by working class people in their own language and for their own purposes. One way to pursue this argument is to quote from a very academic, but nonetheless useful, formulation of the point:

A ruling class will always try to ensure that everybody says and knows what, in practice, the majority do not and *cannot* experience. But that dominated class — and this is the dimension that is overlooked — will experience what it appears cannot be said (at least in public discourse). This makes that experience private, but also immoral, infidel and heathen.

—*From an article by Phil Corrigan and Derek Sayer.*

More simply we can say that the questions of who is to speak, who is to be listened to, and what kinds of voices, and ways of writing are to be valued are always questions of political power as much as they are questions about communication, or education, or literature.

Literary institutions and education

Literature has a privileged status among the arts in Britain: it is something we are known to be good at, we have it so to speak in the bank. English Literature (which artfully subsumes Irish, Welsh and Scottish literature) has been held to embody the best of the humanist traditions that keep the barbarians from the gate. Many of the other arts defer to it by adapting its great works into the other forms: opera, orchestral music, dance, films and television. Yet it is an ancient cry of the artist how obtuse, how satisfied merely to preserve, how unwilling to support new creation, its guardians can be. The banker approach to culture doesn't encourage the granting of overdrafts to today's untried writers.

Training the consumers

This is a struggle that goes on within university literature departments as well as outside; there is a constant resistance to the inclusion of modern works to study, and even when this battle is won, it doesn't necessarily help us or other writers, in that university English is a training in reading, not writing, literature. Even socialist and marxist theories of literature are formed in the university mould and are predominantly theories of criticism, of texts mainly from the past. This is not to be read as a rejection of the work of dead writers. There is no point in writing off Shakespeare, Blake, Jane Austen or Virginia Woolfe as useless because they come from aristocratic or bourgeois traditions. Writers use whoever they can use in their work, and some writers' struggles and victories are recognisable across centuries of cultural change. But a concentration on literature as tradition, as a mode of cultural consumption, is damaging because it rarely focusses on the question of the *production* of contemporary literature – how the literature of today is getting produced and is going to get produced, by whom, in what conditions and with what support.

Three drafts: different people, different periods, same process.
Above: William Blake, *Songs of Experience*.

Crossing The Waste Land.
No. 24.

Crossing the waste land behind the damp
    streets, ~~of the country~~, ~~of F. Edage?~~, October
Crossing the waste land in the ~~autumn~~
    evening,

I thought of T. S. Eliot, and then of

Ianto bach Rees who had never heard of
    T. S. Eliot,

And I saw the dead thistles ~~bend~~ bow to the
    broken tins,

And a jaded pony against the ~~fence~~ crooked fence

Of the bleak allotment.   And I heard

A dozen ~~Thirteen~~ deacons grumbling behind the misty dusk.
    ~~drizzle~~

And the night came down like a ragged flannel shawl

Slowly, slovenly, over the empty ~~streets~~,

And stale ideas lay scattered about the world
    like

Dead horses in a time of famine,
Dead bodies for ~~smart ambitious~~ local ~~collier~~ boys to gaze on

Before they blossomed out as

Saviours of disillusioned men; and then

O ~~Then~~ ~~All~~ the thunder came, and the rains,

~~All~~ the rains came and great was the downpour ~~scream of~~
    ~~the valleys~~, on the chapels and the collieries
And bitter the weeping in the ruins and the cabbages ~~by the mill~~,
Bitter the laughter in the gloom ~~of~~ forsaken Goshen,
And then there was silence, silence.

And the elegant contralto singing by Italian streams
to the third movement sonata in the Miners' Hall.

Idris Davis, 'Crossing the Wasteland', from *Poetry Wales 1981*.

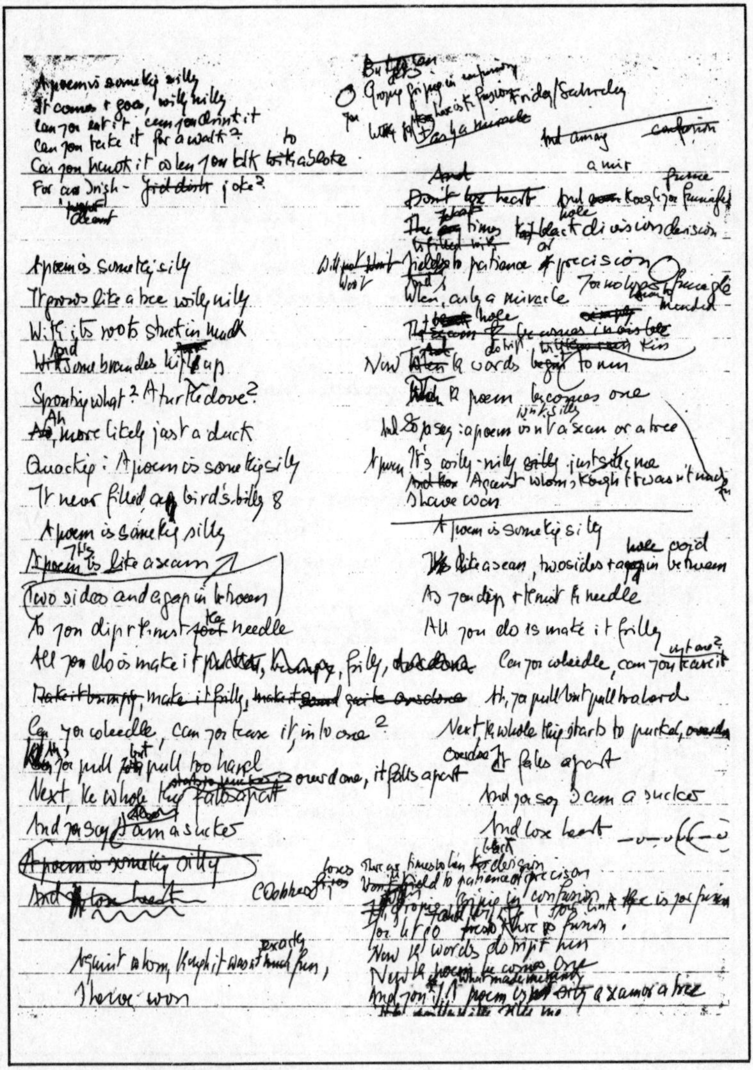
A poem is something silly
It comes & goes, willy nilly
Can you eat it, can you drink it
Can you take it for a walk?
Can you knock it when you talk to a bloke
For an Irish joke?

A poem is something silly
It grows like a tree willy nilly
With its roots stuck in muck
And some branches lift up
Sporting what? A turtledove?
Ah, more likely just a duck
Quacking: A poem is something silly
It never filled a bird's bill
A poem is something silly
It's like a seam
Two sides and a gap in between
As you dip the thread through the needle
All you do is make it frilly
Can you wheedle, can you tease it into one?
If you pull, but pull too hard
Next, the whole thing falls apart
And you say I am a sucker

A poem is something silly
It's like a seam, two sides & a gap in between
As you dip & thread the needle
All you do is make it frilly
Can you wheedle, can you tease it
If you pull but pull too hard
Next, the whole thing starts to pucker
It falls apart
And you say I am a sucker
And lose heart

Lotte Moos, from *Time to be Bold*.

'The Man of Letters'

It's hard to say that there is a prevailing theory of how literature is produced: rather there are bits of theories, or rather assumptions, that between them obscure the real processes of enabling and disabling. There is a bit about individual genius of the romantic kind, which corresponds roughly to the educational proposition that exceptional talent will always find a way through, and that there is enough support available for the few whom it matters to support. (After all, the material resources needed for writing aren't great – just a ball point pen and the backs of some old leaflets.) There is the Man of Letters approach (they usually are men), which combines cultured family, early immersion in literature, probably sedentary job, and suitably learned and cultivated companions – an approach which justifies the real existence of networks based on shared life-styles and the ancient universities. There is the mystification of the writer's work – the tray at the door, the wife fending off phone calls, the morning's work discarded except for the one excellent paragraph – but who rates it excellent? How did the writer get there from his or her first rejection slip? Where has the teaching and learning gone on? The models we have for that are solitary study, the relationship with publisher or editor, or the relationship with a chosen mentor among other writers (the Ezra Pund/T S Eliot connection). What we notably don't hear about is learning from, or with, readers. All the myths, including the hard-nosed modern ones about the commissioning of the best-seller, turn us away from the possibility of teaching or learning to write better.

The skill which cannot be taught?

In this, literature is unique in this country. Those interested in music at schools, playing, composing, making and mixing, can at least compete for the opportunity to go to a full-time college of music. People who have a particular interest in painting, sculpture or other visual arts, can also compete to go to a full-time art college. The same is true of dance, theatre, film-making, television production and so on. The exception is writing. It still seems to be believed that you can either do it or you can't: very little stands between the critical heights of university English, which often convince young writers that the sights are set so high that it's no use trying, and the newspaper ad's 'Make this the year you learn to write'. Among the few exceptional institutions committed to the teachability of writing, or at least to the possibility of a writer's sharing some skills, are the Arvon Foundation and schemes like Writers in Schools. The teaching of creative writing is more widely practised in the USA, often to the scorn of British academia; but it would not be hard to argue that this is a contribution to American literature's being more energetic, less elitist, more open to ethnic and minority experience.

And yet literature *is* organised, there are establishments with the power to damn or to silence or to exclude, without the power to create. This is the old and still justified complaint of other groups as well as worker writers. If we sound stung by the judgements of 'no literary merit', we recognise that we have this in common with many others, just as we recognise that we shouldn't expect to share standards with the literary establishment. The pretence that 'literature will out' whatever the circumstances, acts as a cover for a situation where the 'literary tradition' is in fact readily available only to a few: cultural capital, as well as economic, still moves in restricted circles. It should be easier to confront this from the basis of a view of literature, like other arts, as a mode of cultural production involving formal techniques, learnable processes and styles, and so on. This should make it clearer that we learn different things, recognise different excellence, according to how our learning is shaped and to what ends.

Our project must be aimed, then, both at developing new and more liberating forms of language and culture, and at the development of new and more democratic social relations in which 'literature' is to be produced and consumed. The workshop is a teaching and learning group, evolving with some difficulty to start with, because there are few models for it to build on: what are the ways of helping when you feel a piece of writing could be improved? We should say something here about the teaching of English in schools, as most people have experienced it, and about the relationships that writers and publishing groups have to mainstream education.

Writing in the margins?

We have said earlier that many of the groups have started as adult classes, or otherwise worked in some relation to educational practices or institutions. Characteristically it has been in marginal sectors of education — in remedial classes, supplementary black schools, WEA classes, adult literacy centres, prison education, pensioners' clubs — that writing and people's history have developed. As oppositional activities we could not perhaps expect them to take most hold in the parts of the education system that have most to do with certificating and validating the recognised body of educational and cultural achievements. But the fact that these developments have captured any space at all reflects turbulences within mainstream educational practice and thought. In particular, there were important changes in the teaching of English in schools from the 1960s on. The kinds of writing encouraged in schools widened beyond the socially obsolete form of the essay, on such titles as *A day in the life of an umbrella* or *Bells* or *Those were the days*. This is too wide a development to be adequately covered, but influential figures included David Holbrook with *English for the Rejected* and Ted Hughes who has been a consistent advocate and encourager of children's poetry. It became easier to argue that children had creative power and important matter to write about before they were filled with vocabulary lists and approved sentiments and literary models by the school – that their own lives and experience and sensibilities could shape valuable writing. The other important strand was the debate about the educational significance of issues of language and class, about which we have already written.

They write you off

But it takes a long time to change what is done in schools, and not everybody wants to. These approaches to English teaching came up against two main opponents: those who held that a literature based on students' language and experience was only all right for those who couldn't aspire to *real* standards, as represented by classic literature; and those who held that the appropriate English was that which fitted people for the (mainly obedient and responsive) reading and writing jobs that ordinary life demands, and that self-expression was a luxury and a diversion. Sometimes it was only with the wholly rejected that other relationships and ways of working could be developed. Vivian Usherwood, the young black writer whose wonderful poems were first published by Centerprise in 1972, was a 'remedial' pupil – a demeaning status which, ironically, gave him the time and space to think things out for himself and start writing. His poems have sold over 10,000 copies, many to other young people in Hackney; this makes him one of the best-selling poets of the 1970's, not that you would know it if you read the cultural and literary press. It is sad to mention that Vivian died in a house fire during Christmas 1980.

Billy House and Leslie Mildiner, the joint authors of *The Gates,* found some freedom and encouragement to write and act in the maladjusted school they ended up in after years of truancy. Many young black writers have been encouraged to write in settings outside school or through counter-educational initiatives, such as the Talking Blues group which met at Centerprise, or through the workshops run by the Black Ink project in South London. For young black people there is a particular problem about the language they think and write in. Young black writers like Paul George and Bev Shaw, published by Commonplace Workshop of Ealing, are working through some conscious decisions about using West Indian dialects, standard English, or Black British formations which have grown out of the specific experience of second-generation Black residents. These choices, if they represent independence, can't even with the greatest goodwill be wholly incorporated into the school curriculum. But if the struggle in schools has advanced on any of these issues, it is partly because alternative publishing has produced a body of work to widen the range of models and to keep the debate visible.

Our own institutions

Most older people trying to write now haven't had the benefit of new approaches to English in schools. For them to find an educational setting useful at all, it is often necessary to dismantle the boundaries that seal off education from other parts of life and social action. The Centerprise project in London, for example, was set up in 1971 as an independent initiative which hoped to prove that 'the arts, youth and community work, social work and education itself, are not separate entities invariably requiring separate institutions. They are related and inter-dependent'. Much of Centerprise's early publishing work was done in conjunction with Hackney Workers' Educational Association. Much of the material for, and the editorial work on, its books was provided by a local history class, *A People's Autobiography of Hackney,* and by a writers' workshop, set up after the Federation started, as a piece of direct learning from the Scotland Road and Basement Writers groups. That WEA branch itself was revived after years of non-functioning, as a way of organising a more active and political adult education programme than the highly traditional and non-controversial classes put on year after year by the Adult Education Institute in that area. In using the WEA, people have been responding to, and putting new life into, its traditions of self-organisation, local democracy, and student control of the planning of courses. There have been battles to be won here, for example about the relative merits of academic qualifications, and of local knowledge and informally acquired skill, for the tutor of a class.

The Scotland Road Writers' Workshop came out of a pioneering approach to working class adult education by the Institute of Extension Studies of Liverpool University. The University offered the resources to a group of local people who chose a programme of courses and classes. It is worth mentioning the importance of the decision to appoint to the University's project team someone with the skills to work on writing, as a direct preference to the more predictable radical choice of someone with experience in planning or urban policy. (For further details of the Liverpool experience see the essays by David Evans & M. Yarnit in *Adult Education for a Change,* Hutchinson 1980).

Out of the same set of initiatives has come a 'Second Chance' course that has referred itself deliberately and thoroughly to the situation of working class people, particularly women, as potential students. A local history workshop and a writers' workshop are key parts of this, vital in making it a co-operative rather than a 'taught' course. Several of the Bristol publications, such as *Up Knowle West* and *Bristol as We Remember It,* and also the writers' workshop which produced *Shush, Mum's Writing,* came out of WEA classes. In Southwark, Rochdale, Peckham, Tottenham, Hackney and more recently in Edinburgh, the WEA has played an important role in making education once again a mutual and self-organised project.

The uses of literacy

One of the fields of work where most has to be done to dismantle the old view of learning that many students bring to their new start, is in adult literacy. Here, outstandingly, we are working with a group of people who have built into their understanding of themselves the conviction that they are failures in this activity whose importance isn't in their hands to decide; and who often think they must be punished for failure by a repetition of the rigours and humiliations of their last attempt to learn. It's harder for them to base their study on ideas about sharing in learning, or on a perspective that sees not individual failure but a written culture so hostile that they have been inhibited from freely learning its mechanical skills, though when they do start unpicking their experience of education it produces some compelling writing.

Way of learning

I love to meet entrenched people, mostly friends and family, people like myself. The kind who say, 'Don't spare the rod and spoil the child'. And all that shit. Rules are there to be broken, and break them we did and often. School was a prison, breaking out time at 3.45. That's when we could start to live.

The easy way to beat the system is to cheat by shadow learning: listening, and letting it go over your head. I was good at that. Like sitting at the back of the class, looking out of the window, counting cars, eyeing up girls, having a smoke, or a laugh and a joke. If you were different and didn't understand you were a fool. But you only asked once. You never made that same mistake twice, by becoming the laughing stock of the class. If you asked a question you might make waves and cause people to learn something.

Teachers were there to control the class, holding you at bay until the next lesson. So I made sure I stuck it out, till going home time. With entrenched people, you never prove them wrong. It is easier to let them live in their little world. It's not right, but it's easier. And I know I took the easy way out.

—*Paul Anthony, from 'Listening Ears', Cambridge House/ Blackfriars.*

Turning people's speech into reading matter and showing that spoken language can exist as written language represented a crucial advance in method which led us toward publication of student's work.

These developments took place partly because adult literacy is marginal, under-funded and sketchily organised, so that even at the height of the 'literacy campaign' no major resources were put into the creation of learning materials. It was assumed that the educational publishing market would provide, as it so often is assumed, but it didn't. There was a dead weight of material devised for secondary remedial work, which was soon discarded by most people as transparently irrelevant; but whether we were working from the limited notion of relevance, or from the broader idea that value lies in the greatest possible participation in the creation of the learning material with which you work, the only thing was for students and tutors to do it themselves. It became clear that this was a radical alternative to concepts of functional literacy that not only limited the uses of literacy to those that met bureaucratic requirements, but continued to rule invalid and inadequate the language in which working-class people express, organise and present their lives and understanding.

This way of working had also been encouraged by reports of the work of Paulo Freire in literacy programmes in Brazil. He described not literacy classes but 'culture circles', with the emphasis on mutual education; he saw the professionals' job as being to learn, and then work with, the words that referred to the significant (economically and culturally vital) aspects of people's experience. Through this, both parties to the dialogue learn how people analyse and interpret the world they live in and talk about − in fact, the job for the educator was to show people that they do analyse and interpret the world, and that this is part of their potential power over it.

Producing your own materials

Adult literacy was the first sector of education where the bulk of teaching materials and reading books were autonomously developed by the teachers and students themselves, and distributed nationally through informal and alternative systems. Much of the linking work was done by the group who produced *Write First Time,* a magazine of writing by literacy students, and also a founder member of the Federation. Commercial publishers investigated whether there was a market here for them, but very little was produced − possibly because the scale of the operation was not large enough for their costing systems, and also because they were not close enough to rapidly evolving needs and practices.

But distribution remains a problem for a self-help movement, and here commercial publishers would appear to have a clear advantage. An attempt was made to marry the two systems in a partnership between a national publisher and a literacy centre in Brighton, to produce eight books by Brighton students. Detailed accounts of gains and losses would be hard to draw up, but the gains were expected to include payment for the writers, high quality photographic work, professional illustrations and the assurance of wide sales. However, this has not been the case. Sales are dependent on a marketing department, and while reasonable, have not exceeded those of the best self-help groups. Much of the photographic work was done by a Brighton photographer as was the overall design and layout. Illustrations were twice rejected by two of the editors, who in the end commissioned their own − and one was local. One of the most interesting lessons learned by the group was how limited the photographic and artistic resources of a major publishing house are. Several of the problems were only resolved because of the close personal involvement of the commercial editor who was in sympathy with the ideas behind the group's insistence on controlling the way the text was presented. Nevertheless one is dealing with a corporation, not an individual, and one sympathetic editor cannot manage the whole operation. The worst mistakes were outside his control.

In the final analysis, eight interesting and attractive student written books were made available to other literacy students. It is difficult to assess whether a small under-funded, overworked literacy scheme like the Friends' Centre would have had the time or energy to do all this without the external stimulus. Little money has been made but neither did those involved have the enormous task of seeking finance. Perhaps the most ironic result was that where there were no production difficulties, writers and editors felt far removed and somewhat alienated from the process. The greater the problems, the more the work was referred back to writer and editor, and though the technical production of these sections was perhaps less perfect, the satisfaction of those involved was far greater.

This particular publishing house did at one time consider issuing further student material, but the sympathetic editor has moved on and it now seems unlikely that more such books will be produced by commercial publishers: one series, it seems, has proved to be all that the market will bear.

However, for those involved at all points in the process, with books merely an episode in a chain of communications, learning and and development, there's a different and much less easily satisfied appetite for a great variety of work in a variety of forms. What to the commercial market was the one break-through from below, has been re-absorbed into the thickening foliage that has grown up around it.

It has been essential, for literacy groups as for other groups in the Federation, to learn how to do as much as possible of this work together. Cultural forms and actions till now unaccessible and unrecognised (a meeting to work from talking to writing separately or together; reading over and changing the transcript of a tape; selecting your own and other people's writing for publication; public reading of unpublished or published work) are now among the choices adult students can make.

Our relations to educational establishments and practices mirror our relations to the culture as a whole. We work in margins where we are relatively free from control, but where we often remain insignificant and find it hard to make inroads on the most widely recognised practices. We catch at survivals from the past and re-animate them, borrow from them and pursue the logic of our own developments, hoping out of this to shape something that can assert itself as not of the margin but of the majority, and that can emerge as a substantial culture in its own right.

In the end this brings us, inevitably, to questions of who is to *define* what is 'culture', what is 'good literature' and so on – in short to the questions of the cultural arbiters of our time. In our case the main protagonist in this debate has been the Arts Council of Great Britain.

The guardians of culture

From the beginning, local publishing projects found a genuine interest in their activities from Regional Arts Associations. The Greater London Arts Association was an early financial supporter of the Centerprise publishing project and has remained so; they have also given active support to the later projects around THAP and Peckham Bookplace. Elsewhere in the country this pattern has been repeated; Southern Arts with QueenSpark, NW Arts with Commonword and *Voices*, South West Arts with Bristol Broadsides and so on.

The power to define

At the national level, however, things look very different. The relationship between the Arts Council and the FWWCP is fraught and antagonistic. The battle for recognition and support from this state body has frequently been discussed at Federation meetings. This section explains why that dispute is so crucial.

The struggle over funding and recognition from the Arts Council matters primarily because the development, co-ordination and consolidation of this new movement depends on there being a secure financial basis. The sums of money involved in terms of necessary financial support are relatively small and the question is a valid one of why energy has not been directed towards generating self-sufficiency within the movement, or funding been sought from other sources (effectively the Labour Movement, whose interests surely coincide with those of the Federation itself). If we recognise that the struggle with the Arts Council was never simply about cash we are some way towards an explanation. The Federation, as an organisation and through the writings of its member groups, proposes a re-definition of literature and a challenge to the organisation of literary culture.

For that challenge to be effective it is not enough for groups and individuals to work solely in their localities with small groups of people. This would eventually leave the Federation as an alternative rather than an opposition to the established forms of organisation of Literature.

The Federation had not set out to 'win' writers or readers from high culture, but neither was it winning them for it. It was not about creating the conditions for the one, real writer to emerge and then recommending him or her for individual grant aid. And it was not about fostering the illusion of participatory community arts which, at its worst, composes the bargain basement of the national culture, ephemeral, gaudy and imitative.

The need to be oppositional rather than alternative is part of a much wider political debate which we can only refer to here, but culture plays an important role in maintaining divisive social relations in existence, for the benefit of the ruling class. 'Culture' as defined by its guardians — the spuriously homogeneous national culture — belongs to that minority. The working class is either ignored or misrepresented in that culture. The world it speaks to is not theirs, and access to that culture of the ruling class is available only to the privileged.

If we look at the organisation of the national literary culture, seeing it not as an abstract idea but as a system of power, ownership, control and profit, we realise the degree to which it is sustained by the labour of the working classes. Literature is made from the taxes of working people, distributed as grant aid to writers, just as surely as it is made through their labour in distribution, print processes, publishing and the manufacture of literature's raw materials, paper, pens and ink.

The form in which a national culture develops is neither arbitrary nor natural. Although a state policy for the arts doesn't mean total control over the production of art, it does decide and affirm priorities which, linked to financial support, tend to determine the form in which a particular art will develop and survive. The state policies for the arts also define what is, and is not, within their brief and whether what is matches their criteria.

It is as much the power of definition as the power to allocate financial resources on the basis of those definitions that the Federation contests with the Arts Council.

The Arts Council and the FWWCP

There was early support from the ACGB for one particular form of Federation activity: a grant for £2,000 in 1978 towards the publication of the first national anthology of writing from member groups, *Writing*. It was assumed that this was to be the first stage in what was expected to be a developing relationship as the Federation grew bigger and required more administrative support. For the Literature Panel it was clearly intended to be the first and last. By the time the first major funding application was made to the Panel the Federation was a national movement, albeit at an embryonic stage. In 1978, when the application *to contribute* to the funding of a full-time co-ordinator and certain administrative costs was made, there were around 15 groups scattered across the country, some of whom had been active for a considerable period of time.

Both the Gulbenkian Trust and the Arts Council were approached at the same time with an outline of a three year scheme to employ a full-time national co-ordinator, together with administrative and travelling costs, and a smaller amount to pay for members to travel to national meetings. The amount in question was quite modest, about £7,500 per annum for three years. Talks were held at which representatives from Gulbenkian, the Literature Director of the ACGB and members of the Federation were present. Gulbenkian were very keen as they saw the growth of the local publishing movement as a part of the new community initiatives they were keen to support. The Literature Director of the Arts Council was markedly less enthusiastic. Right from the beginning it was obvious that the Arts Council, through their officers, regarded the local publishing and writers' workshop movement as a phenomenon quite unconnected with 'literature' and probably something to do with all that community politics stuff, a lot of ghastly frothing about on council estates which are certainly not the kind of places to go looking for *literature*.

'Not good writing...'

They suggested a meeting, held in March 1979, which was, we were told, almost withour precedent. Applicants rarely meet the panel. It was a very hostile occasion indeed. We didn't even realise at the time that it wasn't the Literature Panel we were meeting but the Finance Committee of the Panel. Amongst the comments made were that such local publications were 'interesting, possibly, from a sociological view', but unfortunately, however interesting these little books might be they were 'not good writing'; that the Federation's emphasis on the working class experience was 'racialist' (sic), and that such quaint little local projects might be deformed and spoilt by national co-ordination. This was followed up with a letter declining to assist the Federation:

There is no doubt in the minds of the Committee that on a community level the work is of sound value and... a new reading public is responding to this situation. Nevertheless... no recommendation for grant-aid from the Literature budget can be forthcoming. The members were in one voice in judging the examples of literature submitted: they considered the whole corpus of little, if any, solid literary merit, and, therefore — sympathetic as they are to the community value of the Federation — cannot feel justified in recommending grant-aid from the Literature allocation of funds. Two members of the Committee also felt strongly that there was little point in organising the groups of the Federation on a national basis: they felt the whole strength of the work lay in its stimulation of local activities and interests, and in binding the people of a certain locality together by virtue of those common interests... After long discussion it was agreed that the only action which might bear fruit is once again to direct your application to the Community Arts Committee of the Council...

Fighting talk indeed. Their decision not to fund the Federation is clarified by Jim McGuigan, a sociologist who was present at the time in the course of researching the Literature Panel's system of grant-aid to writers. His report, when published, had all detailed references to the Federation and its application meticulously deleted. This is what he had written about the meeting described above:

After the Federation representatives had left the meeting a lengthy discussion took place between the committee members. Apart from the chairman, the committee was opposed to assisting the Federation. Melvyn Bragg said he was not impressed by the writing but thought the Federation was doing a good job by encouraging working class people to read literature. He offered a compromise solution: an initial grant of £6,000 and after a year appraisal of the continuing work of the Federation before giving more assistance. This was rejected by the rest of the Finance Committee... Charles Osborne explained the views of the Literature Finance Committee to me:

'The kind of writing which they were encouraging into publication didn't really for the most part justify itself on literary grounds... One could see it was useful from a therapeutic point of view, perhaps, and maybe in general social terms, community terms, for people whose writing talents might be quite modest to encourage them to write if it was of use to them, and sometimes a lot of the things were interesting to people in the immediate vicinity... There wasn't, we thought, a great deal, or indeed very much at all they were producing which was at all sort of justifiable in terms of literary merit which wouldn't get published in the more normal kind of way because it was worth publishing. But we could see there was perhaps a case to be made out for them as performing a useful sort of social function. And we thought if they were going to get any Arts Council money at all they would be more likely to get it from our Community Arts sort of people.'

The Gulbenkian Foundation, who had been particularly keen to enter into joint funding with the Arts Council, generously went ahead with the first year of the three year funding programme. A full-time worker was appointed. At the same time another letter was written to the Arts Council asking them to consider taking over the second year's funding. This led to an interesting correspondence in which we learnt a great deal about the assumptions concerning literature, culture and politics held by the guardians and paymasters of British cultural development.

The glittering prizes

The next occasion on which it was possible to raise these issues in public came in March 1980 when the Literature Panel called a public forum to discuss the work of the Panel. It was an invitation-only occasion (even their definition of 'public forum' is askew) and the Federation put a lot of hard work into securing three tickets. Though all questions had to be submitted in writing in advance it should have been a lively and controversial occasion. It was neither. The only thing that sparkled was the ornate chandelier suspended in the middle of the plush conference room.

The evening got off to an unpromising start with the embarrassing realisation that hardly any of the members of the Panel itself had managed to turn up to take part in this rare occasion at which their policies could be questioned and discussed. This confirmed the all-pervasive influence of the full-time Literature Director who replied in person to every question. The fact that Literature only gets 1.2% of the Arts Council budget, a percentage which continues to get smaller each year, was unconvincingly explained away as being due to there being no massive loss-making organisations in Literature, unlike Covent Garden for the Music Panel or the National Theatre for Drama. They refused our request to be considered their big loss-making organisation as they had no other. But the Director then went on to rub salt in the wounds of the assembled public by saying that the Panel *could* get more money, but the fact was that there weren't enough applications of sufficient literary merit to warrant making available extra funds.

The work of the local publishing movement was dismissed gently with the comment that interesting though this writing by taxi-drivers and coloured school-children was, it had failed to convince the Literature Panel members of its eligibility for a grant.

They then went on to announce more major prizes, three new prizes of £7,500 for poetry, fiction and criticism, with three judges to be paid £2,000 each for assessing the literary merit amongst the entries. Not one woman's voice was heard that evening; there was no mention of the major significance of contemporary feminist writing, or of the African, Caribbean and young black British contribution to the energy of post-war literature published in Britain.

As people were leaving, the Federation members were approached by one of the two Literature Panel members who did show up who said how interested he was to learn of the activities of the Federation. He also claimed that he had never seen or even heard of our application. Which confirmed our belief that substantial screening processes are employed before lay members of the Panel actually get a chance to have their say.

Greg Wilkinson of the Commonword Workshop, who attended the meeting, wrote afterwards to Sir Roy Shaw, Secretary General, re-stating the Federation's case:

In answer to your own remarks, the point is not that an occasional taxi-driver or black schoolboy should have a piece picked for the prize-giving, nor that our movement − comprising hundreds of working men and women who write − is mainly concerned with merit awards... What matters is that a lot of writers who have not been educated or mesmerised into a certain literary convention − but whose experience, feeling and imagination is all the more notable for that − must now make do without the support that your Literature budget, and our tax money, could well provide.

How long can we divorce 'literary merit' from the life and people that literature should represent and transform? Can we accept that the great majority of working men and women should rely on those who love and leave them to write on their behalf, while what they write themselves is disregarded? Can we accept that there is just one Literature and set standards for all, and that these should be fixed by a little minority, who, in refining their writing skills to the standards of a relatively leisured class, remove themselves from the life and language of the majority?

We want the chance to develop our own standards, standards possible and intelligible to people who work long, un-intellectual, ill-paid hours; to people whose intelligence cannot be simply highjacked from the circumstances − the scope and the limitations − they share with most of the un-Literary public. These circumstances may not favour the codes and constructs of conventional Literature, but they may evoke new forms more fitted to a content that Literature largely ignores (or older forms) that the Literature of the day has overlaid: where would even classical music be today if jazz had not emerged, or sculpture without the 'primitive' works 'discovered' by people like Epstein; and do we have to go as far as Africa or the Deep South to recognise the limitations of our little, local, and class, standards? Have the greater part of our own people got nothing to offer to a Greater Literature?

As for the Worker Writers' movement, this is not some therapeutic sideline to be nodded off to Community Arts (and we find it hard to accept the whole notion of a two-tier system, implicit in Community Arts; a sort of jumble sale or bargain basement, where prices and distinctions are slashed, where everything is possible and all mixed up as long as it's cheap).

Amateurs and professionals: gentlemen and players

The comparison between literature and music is interesting, because music is the other cultural form in which many of the same crass divisions and distinctions as are made about literature are also used. For, whilst Opera and Symphony Orchestras are given some £13 million a year, the money available for jazz, experimental rock and folk music is negligible. In fact folk music is said by some members of the Music Panel not to count in its terms of reference. The English Folksong and Dance Society is actually funded by the Sports Council! A large part of the case against folk music is that it is largely the province of 'amateurs', an argument that has also been used for not funding the Federation, another cultural province of 'amateurs'. Whilst supporting the rights of professional cultural workers to good living standards and proper working conditions, we do feel that this should not be seen as therefore permanently maintaining the distinction between 'amateurs' and 'professionals' as in all other areas of our lives. The 'amateurs' argument was the one used, interestingly, in reply to the TUC letter supporting the Federation's case for funds; the ACGB clearly thought that was a good hand to play when dealing with the trade union movement.

The wisdom of the impeccable heavenly democrat

A woman active in the 'Women and Words' workshop in Birmingham wrote to the Literature Director criticising the decision not to fund the Federation and questioning the right of the committee to decide on what had 'insufficient literary merit' without explaining what their criteria were. The reply illuminated even further the Arts Council's thinking about writers and reading publics:

It may seem unfair to you that some people are more talented than others, and indeed it is unfair; however, it remains a fact that talent in the arts has not been handed out equally by some impeccable heavenly democrat. You are right to think that the Arts Council views itself as a patron of the arts. This is, indeed, our function. It is important that we do all we can to increase audiences for today's writers, *not that we increase the number of writers.* There are already too many writers chasing too few readers. Although the real writer will always emerge without coaxing, it is not so easy to encourage new readers into existence! (Our italics)

The Arts Council justified its refusal of grant-aid primarily on the basis that the work produced by the member groups was 'of insufficient literary merit'. Were it not for the power which this undefined and undefinable term exerts it would be a laughable response to the varied writings of the worker writer movement and the detailed, well argued case for funding put forward and matched by an impressive array of support from inside and outside the FWWCP.

The charge of 'insufficient literary merit' is clearly the safest and most effective objection to the work of the FWWCP. On the question of funding the FWWCP, the Arts Council is contradictory. The discrepancy between Regional Arts Associations (who have contributed to virtually every member group within the Federation) and the national policy can only partly be explained by the conflicts between regional and national organisation. The nub of the contradiction is that it was an Arts Council grant that enabled *Writing,* the first national anthology of the movement *as a movement,* to be published.

What this contradiction points to is that the charge of 'insufficient literary merit' is far from being the whole story. The Arts Council refuses to discuss what it means by literary merit, nor will they disclose how standards are agreed and their judgements arrived at.

Jim McGuigan is again illuminating on this:

Although criteria of evaluation were not made explicit in the finance committee, members seemed to understand what each other meant when terms like 'merit', 'quality' and 'serious' were used. The concept of 'serious writing' is crucial to the decision making.

Melvyn Bragg, in discussion with Jim McGuigan, had this to say:

I think serious writing is represented by those people who think that they represent it at the time... the Arts Council Literature Panel is full of people who could be said to either be writing or representing serious literature in various ways.

Asked if he considered 'literary merit' to be a definable concept he replied:

I don't think so. I mean you could theorise about it. I'm not inclined to.

The discussion and debate on questions of literary merit, values, standards and quality which took place within the Federation and its member groups as a result of this judgement were, on the whole, a valuable contribution to its work. Attempts to debate the matter with the Arts Council were fruitless from our point of view but perhaps for them it was a successful ploy. People were kept occupied with a question conveniently irrelevant to the real issue. By running the hare of literary merit they made it impossible to turn discussion (where it took place at all) onto the dangerous area of the power of institutions and the control, production and uses of literature.

There are two basic explanations for why the Arts Council will support what it takes to be a one-off collection of *writing* but refuse support to an institutional base for the development of that writing. One lies in the stated policy towards support for literature set out in their charter and subsequent policy documents. The second concerns the composition and mode of operation of the Arts Council itself and the determining effect this has on the interpretation and subsequent implementation of those policies. We will consider each in turn.

An empty golden treasury

Literature claims just over 1% of the total Arts Council budget. Between 1946, when the Arts Council received its Royal Charter, and 1966, when 'A Policy for the Arts' was adopted, there was no formal commitment to literature. This is a testimony not to literature's marginality but to its ability to manage itself. The centrality of 'English' to the school curriculum, the existence of a free public library system and the commercial viability and expansion of publishing rendered state support for literature (as opposed to the minority art of poetry) unnecessary.

When a Literature Panel and a financial budget was established, its role was primarily conceived in terms of grant-aid to individual writers. Despite very cogent arguments to the contrary, aid to already established writers as individuals continues to be the keystone of state policy towards literature.

Some of the most powerful and consistent criticisms of the Arts Council policy towards literature at the time of its formulation were to be found in the pages of the *Times Literary Supplement*. The main concern was that in 'its concern with the blooms' at the expense of the 'roots and branches' the Arts Council was neglecting 'the actual basis of our literature' and contributing nothing to its growth and development.

The Arts Council's answer to these criticisms followed what

seems to be its standard response to criticism: it ranged from silence to evasion of the issues involved. Despite this, the Literature Panel's involvement in areas other than direct grant-aid to individual writers has increased over the years. There is, however, a clear residual commitment to the individual writer and to the known, rather than emergent, writer at that. When confronted with a movement within literature, even to some extent *against* literature, Charles Osborne, then Director of the Literature Panel, can only respond in individual terms; a concern with 'the writer' rather than with writing.

The writer or the writing?

The Federation's case has never rested on individuals – as readers or as writers. Its concern has been to develop an institutional form which can accommodate the actual and potential attitudes and relations to writing held by the working class of this country. Furthermore, even as the policy for state support begins to shift from the individual writer to the apparatus of literary culture, it retains an exclusive focus on the literary magazines, small presses, and forms of publishing subsidy which characterise the predominance of the metropolitan white middle classes within the national literary culture.

The change in emphasis in the Arts Council's activities, particularly innovations such as Writers' Tours, Creative Writing Fellowships and Writers in Schools, indicates a shift away from the view of the writer as an isolated individual who writes, to that of the writer as a person who must generate – or have generated for him/her – an audience for their work. The emphasis moves from the primary production of literature to the education of the consumer:

We need to do something about the arts, because they are undersubsidised, underpatronised, undervalued and, if I may coin a word, underdistributed. —ACGB Bulletin March 1980 – Roy Shaw.

The professional, privileged status of the writer is maintained. It is not the *activity of writing* that generates interest in literature, but *the writer*. Ted Hughes, Douglas Dunn and Susan Hill are felt to do the job of encouraging school children's interest in writing far better than an average English teacher, and this reinforces the distinction between writers and people who write which appeared to be breaking down with the adoption of progressive English teaching. The principle informing the Federation's approach to reading and writing, that you are both a producer and a consumer of writing, and that your skills in relation to each are mutually benefitting and intermeshed, is inevitably incomprehensible within this scheme.

The producers, who are of necessity few, remain distinct from the consumers, of whom there are never enough.

There are already too many writers...

What ensures that the Federation cannot benefit from this policy change is the implicit assumption about who can benefit from this strategy towards the 'consumer'. It is young people, primarily young middle class people within the education system, and mainly in further and higher education who are to benefit. The Federation is composed largely of adults, many of whom received the minimum of formal education. Although at particular points it stands in a close relation to 'education' – through literacy work, through the WEA, through 2nd Chance Adult Education – its aims are not primarily educational. It is not compensatory, it does not seek to impose standard English and conventional literary values, it does not seek to improve people's 'English'. Thus, in relation to the Arts Council, the Federation lacks a primary commitment to educational work, and the people with whom it has (or is likely to have) contact are considered to lack potential for literary excellence as producers or literary competence as readers. Putting money into the Federation would be, in the Arts Council's terms, an investment without return.

It is for this reason that the achievement of generating involvement with reading and writing represented by the sales, publications and readings record of the Federation's member groups can be overlooked in the concern to generate new audiences.

It is important that we do all we can to increase audiences for today's writers, not that we increase the number of writers. There are already too many writers chasing too few readers. Although the real writer will always emerge without coaxing, it is not so easy to encourage new readers into existence.

It would appear that it is not simply readers that are required but a certain kind of reader to complement – indeed to read – the 'real' writers.

We can see how the actual policy guidelines within which the Literature Panel operates are framed in such a way as to marginalise the intentions, work and achievements of the Federation. This marginality is compounded when we consider the composition of the Arts Council Literature Panel and its procedures. This has been discussed by Raymond Williams in an article *The Arts Council* which he wrote after serving as a panel member.

A little bit of democracy is a good thing

Raymond Williams's main argument is that the Arts Council *appears* to be:

An intermediate body, responsibly and accountably disposing of public money and including in itself people with direct current knowledge of the arts and their administration.

In reality, however, the social processes through which it works produce only marginal independence; its budgets and its appointments are the work of government ministers, its decision-taking consensual and co-optive (viz the sacking of Richard Hoggart).

The procedures of the council flow from fundamental assumptions... embodied in its mode of appointment and constitution. What begins, from a department of state, as a process of selective and administered consensus, cannot become... an open and democratic public body.

Decisions are effectively taken by full-time officers of the Arts Council, not its 'representative' lay members.

They sit... around the council table with lay members. In practice I would say policies are determined by these officers and the panel chairman, in consultation where necessary with the council chairman and the council's senior officers. The... lay council, and even more the lay panels, come through as interested occasional parties, though the consensual mood encourages them to see themselves, and... to be generally seen, as a fully responsible public body.

This lack of democracy and public accountability means that dissent and debate — of whatever kind — are 'managed' rather than harnessed to progress.

The Literature Panel doubtless considers itself to be a rock of stable quality and excellence within the choppy waters of cultural change. Others take a more cynical view of their policies in practice:

A striking feature of the system of Grants to Writers is the interchangeability of roles: grant recipient/sponsor/panel member... During their period of service, Panel members are not eligible for assistance. However, grant recipients are not excluded from subsequently becoming Panel members, nor are former Panel members ineligible for grants. Since 1966 sixteen individuals have received grants either before or after serving on the panel. Perhaps this is not surprising. However, it does provide further evidence of the regularised interconnections between grant giver and receiver.   —Writers and the Arts Council — Jim McGuigan

Members of the Federation felt particularly slighted on learning that the details of their submission were unknown to many members of the Literature Panel. It would seem, though, that this ignorance of the cases under their consideration is quite usual, particularly when we take into account the advisory nature of the Panel. The real decisions are taken by a Finance Committee.

This account so far seems very depressing. In fact, the Federation won a partial victory over the Arts Council in getting money to fund a part-time 'Literature Development Officer'. In addition, the recognition and support from the Gulbenkian Foundation, the contact with the TUC Education Advisory Committee, the favourable coverage by Press and television, and the actual growth of the movement itself all testify to some degree of changing awareness. Although the Federation does have curiosity value for some sections of the media, it became clear through the struggle with the Arts Council that the solid case made by the Federation was recognised and supported by a wide range of institutions and individuals, not all of whom are necessarily committed to its aims or the politics it tends to represent. The Arts Council began to look increasingly foolish, and the occasion of the change of chairmanship of the Literature Panel, from Melvyn Bragg to Marganita Laski, provided an opportunity for them to back track as well as to save face.

Institutions of labour

Naturally the Federation will continue to seek financial support from the Literature Panel of the Arts Council, not through any wish to obtain approval or legitimation from the state, but simply because we feel that, since money has been paid by working people out of their taxes, we have a right to have some of it back for the work we are involved in. Yet we also wish to secure for the Federation and the activities of its members groups, serious financial support from the trade union movement. We do feel that the kind of history-making, autobiography writing and poetry and short story writing practised in Federation groups comes from a background which is also the home of past and present trades unionism. The range of themes explored in people's writings described earlier relates very closely to the constituency and interests of working people. Already some trade unions have shown an interest in this field. The TGWU monthly paper, *The Record*, has devoted its central pages for some years to poetry and short stories written by its members. NUPE districts have on occasion run poetry competitions, the entries to which the Federation magazine, *Voices*, has recently published as a selection. The NUR set what could be a very important precedent, by giving Joe Smythe paid leave to write his poetry collection *The People's Road*. We hope this increasing interest will quite soon lead to firmer links between the trade unions and the Federation.

Another indication of this interest came from the TUC Working Party Report on *The Arts* which acknowledged the new role played by many local publishing groups in working people's lives:

The establishment, in certain areas, of local publishing houses... is very much welcomed by the working party. Local authorities could do a great deal to stimulate writing in their various localities, by encouraging community publications. They should also be conscious that very little creative writing by working class authors has in the past survived and when diaries, reminiscences and essays giving a view of the world as working people see it are discovered, historians value them highly.

These days, of course, it no longer has to be just historians who might gain access to such documents and writings. We have the material means of production for making these available to a wide audience as and when they are written.

We strongly hope then that the TUC Advisory Committee on the Arts, Entertainment and Sports, which was set up as a result of the 1976 Report, will address itself to the arguments in this book and urge both the TUC itself and individual trade unions to support the creative capacities of their members by financially supporting the Federation, member groups and individual writers, in order that the writing and publishing movement can expand even further and create a genuine history and literature of working people in Britain.

We also strongly urge the Labour Party to make the encouragement and financial support of the writers' movement a priority in its policy-making statements and discussions on local government policies for the arts. Its own policy document *The Arts and the People* which came out in 1977, a year after the TUC document, is weak in its awareness of the powerful movement represented by the Federation and is also simply wrong on some of the facts. In the section on bookshops it attributes the development of the community bookshop movement to the Arts Council, when in fact the opposite process was the case. Generous the Arts Council has certainly been to several such bookshops in recent years (bookshops initiated locally and often sustained in their first years by one or two paid workers and hundreds of hours of voluntary help), but it has yet to issue a public policy statement on financial support for bookshops.

State support, yes, but not municipal literature

We contest both the language and the definitions of the Labour Party document in its characterisation of 'literature as a community art form' and its differentiation between 'amateur' writing and that of professionals, not just as a difference of payment and non-payment but in the status of the writing itself.

The Labour Party is clearly right in its concern for the proper financial remuneration of commercially published writers and its support for the policies of the Writers' Guild, but surely (together with the trade unions) it should examine ways in which working people could obtain paid leave and grants to write. Their suggestion of 'Direct state intervention in the shape of a state publishing house, with regional branches...' ignores the reality of the situation. Over the past ten years many such regional and local publishing initiatives have been set up and run successfully on a self-organised and co-operative basis. Now, while there may be a place for a non-commercial national publishing house, we feel that local and regional needs can be catered for by initiatives such as already exist within the Federation — with additional funds being, of course, greatly welcomed.

The arguments here run in parallel with those raised in recent years about the labour movement's best response to unfavourable coverage in the mass media. One line of argument suggests that the problems can be best dealt with by the launching of a new Labour sponsored national daily paper which would provide sympathetic coverage. But against this it can be said that there are already, in different parts of the country, a number of 'alternative' and socialist local papers, and that the best strategy is to support and develop these local initiatives while respecting their autonomy.

A state publishing house, like a sponsored Labour daily or a subsidised national printing resource, might very quickly ossify into a bureaucracy functioning to reproduce a state 'programme' of pre-conceived 'solutions' and ideas.

The first necessity is to support and develop the local projects that already exist, where new voices are telling their own stories, articulating their own demands and desires. It is the development of this process, through which new voices are beginning to be heard, which is the priority. We cannot prejudge what the voices will say, nor expect them to conform to some pre-defined 'correct' perspective, nor can we yet know what might be accepted as solutions to problems only now becoming recognised and defined. But, as the writing, poetry and autobiography develops, what is clear is the vitality and urgency of this movement still in movement as these words are set in print.

Writers' workshops/ community publishers: List of member groups

The descriptions of the activities of the various groups listed below were compiled on the basis of replies to a list of questions about their work which we sent out to all the groups we knew of. Where no reply was received at the time of going to press we have simply given a brief outline of the groups concerns, or in some cases, simply a contact address.

FEDERATION OF WORKER WRITERS AND COMMUNITY PUBLISHERS *6 Twiss St, Liverpool 8.*

This is the address to contact for more information about the FWWCP and its activities — please enclose a stamped, addressed envelope with all enquiries.

The Federation's first anthology of writing by member groups, *Writing,* is still available for £1.75 (including postage) from FWWCP c/o 76 Carysfort Rd, London, N16.

BASEMENT WRITERS
Old Town Hall, Cable St. E1

A writer's workshop which meets on a weekly basis.

BRISTOL BROADSIDES
110 Cheltenham Rd, Bristol BS6 5RW   0272-40491

Bristol Broadsides is a co-operative publishing group which was set up in 1977. We have about 20 members, age range between twenties and sixties and a more or less equal number of women and men. We have produced eleven publications including *Bristol as We Remember It, Shush Mum's Writing, Toby,* and *Tears and Joy.* Many of our books have come either from writers' workshops or history groups — which we run in conjunction with the WEA. At present (Jan 82) we have three writers' workshops running in Bristol.

We are given a grant by South West Arts to pay the salary of a full time worker. The production costs and overheads are financed out of sales; with the help of grants from such organisations as Bristol City Council and the Mental Health Foundation — who helped fund *Tears and Joy.*

CENTERPRISE PUBLISHING PROJECT
136 Kingsland High St, London E8   01-254-9632

Publishing from Centerprise bookshop/Community centre, in conjunction with Hackney People's Autobiography and Writers' Workshop groups (see below). The project has published over 40 titles since 1973, including poetry, prose and pictures, local history, autobiography and fiction. Write for current list.

COMMONPLACE WORKSHOP
28 Dorset Rd, Ealing, London W5

The workshop has existed since 1975 and has 6 publications to date, the last of which was published in Sept. 1981. Several different writers' groups have met during this time. The current group is all women and meets fortnightly. We are about 10 in number, and range in age from late 20's to 76. The workshop started with the publication of an anthology of poetry written by four young women living in Southall. Later on the first writers' group began to meet. We receive no financial support and fund-raise locally by putting on plays, shows, poetry readings, etc.

COMMONWORD WRITERS' WORKSHOP
61 Bloom St, Manchester M1 3LY   061-236-2773

Commonword began after an oral history project in the overspill town of Partington. It was decided to start a group not just for autobiography, but for a wide range of working class writers. This began meeting in the centre of Manchester in 1977. After initial funding from Job Creation, we were given grants from the council and the local arts association to employ workers, develop writers' workshops and put out publications.

The group draws in people from all around Manchester, with representatives of all ages and backgrounds. From the start, however, there've been very few women members. This has been put down to various factors, including the fact that men in groups act very differently to women, and that women felt unable to read out work that was often very personal. At the end of 1979, an all women's group, Home Truths, was set up in Stretford Library, to be followed, in 1981, by another women's group (this time a daytime one) in Longsight Neighbourhood Centre. (*Mum's the Word!*) Another group was started in 1981 for children in Stretford, *The Write Crowd*, and we are also involved with Rochdale Writers' Group.

Over the years, we've become more and more ambitious with our publications, and we have our own press. An anthology in 1977, *Coming Up*, was followed by our quarterly magazine, *Write On*. Other publications include poetry by four early Commonword poets(*Commonverse*), and poetry by Joe Smythe and Joan Batchelor (*Come and Get Me, On the Wild Side*). Our most widely read book is probably *Clout!,* in which battered women talk about their lives. *Dobroyed* is an autobiographical novel, written in its own spelling and virtually its own language, about a young boy's life in approved school, and *Home Truths* is an anthology of women's writing. Our most recent publications are *Nothing Bad Said*, the first short story collection to be published by a worker writer group; and *In All Innocence* – poems by Stan Preston.

All these groups meet weekly or fortnightly. Most of them began with two or three members, but we now include dozens of writers under the Commonword banner.

EAST BOWLING HISTORY WORKSHOP
75 Brompton Rd, Bradford BD4 7JE

GATEHOUSE PROJECT
St. Luke's, Sawley Rd, Miles Platting, Manchester 10   061-205-9522
The Gatehouse Project has been in existence since November 1977 and is based in north Manchester. The Project's writing and publishing workshops are all with adults whose initial involvement has come through adult literacy classes. In the last four years it has published 11 books, all of them written or taped by people learning to read and write.
Three writing workshops are meeting regularly at present. These are 'Tip Of My Tongue', a women's writing group meeting weekly at our premises in Miles Platting and with an average attendance of 5-7, a Hulme writers' workshop which also meets weekly and involves approximately 14 students on a TSD Preparatory Course, and an editorial/writing group in south Manchester which meets fortnightly. All these groups are working on collections of writing, soon to be published.
We also run short-term writing workshops of three sessions. We have so far worked with sixty groups, each workshop culminating in the production of a magazine by the group. The three sessions – writing, editing/illustrating and layout – cover the various stages involved in the writing and publishing of ideas, our aim being to de-mystify the process by which words get into print. We hope that having been through the process with us, groups will feel able to go on and produce their own reading material.
The Project is funded by the Inner City Programme and has three workers. Books are fund-raised for individually.

HACKNEY WRITERS' WORKSHOP
c/o Centerprise, 136 Kingsland High Street, London E8
The workshop was started in 1976 as a WEA class based at Centerprise. Over the last five years some 30 people have been involved in the workshop, and meetings have usually averaged an attendance of 8-10. We have produced three anthologies of work which we collected, discussed, edited and designed and pasted-up ourselves, as a group.
Members have been involved in giving readings in pubs, adult education classes, literacy conferences, in associations with local political and cultural campaigns, and have also given a reading in a prison. The age range has run from 16 to 76, with an equal number of women and of men.

LIVERPOOL 8 WRITERS' WORKSHOP
6 Twiss St, Liverpool 8
The group, which was formed in 1975 is mixed as between black and white, old and young, and is 2/3 male, 1/3 female. The work produced is mainly about where we are at politically, socially and economically. An occasional love poem or short story (of pure imagination) arises, and is of course welcome. There is a hard core of about 15 members who turn up every week. We have produced two magazines and are getting started on a third. Our interest in performing our work live to any audience that will listen has always been keenly felt. Some say we will perform at the drop of a hat. We have very close links with all the other Liverpool groups.
We have no source of finance, except when we have occasionally applied to any Trust with a few pounds to spare, and only then when we have needed to produce a magazine. In fact we, like the rest of Liverpool 8, live very

much hand to mouth – but we survive: though in the past we have had small amounts of money from Merseyside Community Relations, Partnership and the Liverpool Adult Education Consortium.

LONDON VOICES POETRY/PROSE WORKSHOP
70 Holden Rd, Woodside Park, London N12 7DY

The group originally formed in 1974 in order to help promote the *Voices* magazine which is published in Manchester, and transformed itself into a writers' workshop in 1979. The group comprises 8-12 people, equal as between men and women, people of all ages, and meets monthly. Publications include *There's None Ever Feared* 1978; bi-monthly broadsheets, and an anthology is in preparation. People come to the workshop from all over London. The group is self-financing, although they do now have sponsorship from the Co-op. Members have given poetry readings for CND, cultural festivals, etc.

NETHERLEY & DISTRICT WRITERS' WORKSHOP
38 Glebe Hey, Netherley, Liverpool 27

The group was established in 1978 with 3 women and one child. The child wrote the first poem for our book. We produced this within a few months as the workshop seemed to become instantly popular. People who didn't want to write contributed by having meetings in their homes, or helping design the cover, etc. The workshop now meets weekly, with an average attendance of 6 people. The age range is from 10 to approx. 55, with an equal number of men and women, though in the past it was nearly all women. We are all local people, and have published 3 books, and are in the process of publishing a fourth. We financed our first book by a few members missing a week's rent. The proceeds have paid for the following publications. That is all the finance we have.

We are all people who either live in Netherley or have friends here. We are interested in the writings of working class people and the history of the working class – which we know is not a purely individual characteristic. But we do feel that we are one of the few groups who have started themselves and not been started by a tutor or middle class writer, and who get no financial assistance from anyone. We like that as we can please ourselves what we write and we don't have to answer to anyone.

OLD SWAN WRITERS' WORKSHOP
30 Fieldway, Liverpool 15

The workshop was established in 1979 in Old Swan Technical College as part of the Adult and Community Education programme. The group has a paid tutor/co-ordinator, but we hope eventually to sever our links with the college and meet elsewhere. We meet on each Wednesday evening during term time, and fortnightly in members' houses, during the summer. The average attendance is about 10 people, although members often bring guests with them. There seem to be equal numbers of men and women attending, with an age-range between 17 and 83; young children occasionally bring their work to us too.

To date we have published 3 anthologies of work: *Ring of Words; Swan Song (1)* and *Swan Song (2)*. At present we are working on a fourth, more satirical booklet, provisionally titled *Spit It Out*. The first three books were duplicated on college equipment, but our fourth will be printed on an offset-litho machine, belonging to the workshop, and bought with an £800 grant from Merseyside Arts Association.

We are still establishing contacts with the local community mostly through giving readings, word-of-mouth and by printing leaflets for local groups on our printing press. Collectively we represent a wide range of interests: drama, CND, feminism, 'Free Radio', and local history, to name but a few.

PECKHAM PUBLISHING PROJECT
The Bookplace, 13 Peckham High St, London SE15   01-701-1757

Peckham Publishing Project started in 1977. It aims to produce books by and for people in Southwark as an integral part of work at The Bookplace, Peckham's community bookshop. It is run by the Publishing Group and a full-time Bookplace worker. The group has regular monthly meetings to make decisions. Work sessions on individual books are organised as necessary. The members are local people from a wide range of cultural backgrounds and occupations and there are close ties with the Peckham Writers, Peckham People's History and The Bookplace Education Project. To March '82, twelve books have been published, with particular emphasis on writing by women, school students, black people and old people. The project is non-profit-making and aims to be financially self-sufficient. Books are priced as cheaply as possible to cover printing costs and overheads. Writers receive no royalties and retain copyright of their work. Financial support comes from the Greater London Arts Association and other organisations like Southwark Libraries, the Equal Opportunities Commission and the John Collett Trust, which help with grants or interest-free loans for specific publications. Publishing policy is actively anti-racist, anti-sexist and anti-fascist and open to all local people on this basis.

PECKHAM WRITERS
The Bookplace, 13 Peckham High St, London SE15   01-701-1757

The Peckham Writers began as a group in 1978. They meet every Tuesday evening from 7.30-9.30. Around ten people usually come, women and men, representing a cross-section of multi-cultural Southwark. They are mostly in their twenties or early thirties, though there is a strong policy of keeping the group open to all. They have published three anthologies of members' work, including *Person to Person* in 1982. There are also periodical newsletters. The Writers have good relations with the Peckham Publishing Project, sharing material, publishing skills and decision-making. The Writers have a small publishing grant from the Publishing Project for their own publications. Recently they have begun to go into schools to read poems and stories, as well as appearing at local and FWWCP events.

PEOPLE'S PUBLICATIONS
34 Fenham Rd, Newcastle on Tyne NE4 5PB   09632 761351

QUEENSPARK BOOKS
13 West Drive, Brighton, Sussex   0273 682855

A community newspaper group that moved – via local history features – into books.

SCOTLAND ROAD WRITERS' WORKSHOP
113 Byrom Street, Liverpool 3

A working class Liverpool group based at the Vauxhall Community Centre. The first known writers' workshop of the 70's revival, this group was formed in 1972.

SE1 PEOPLE'S HISTORY GROUP
10 Brief St, London SE5 9RD   01-274-4617

SE1 People's History Group was formed in January 1979; in the April it became a WEA class. It meets regularly and has an average attendance of about ten with an age range spanning thirty to eighty comprising slightly more women than men.

Besides meeting as a class the convenor is paid for a couple of hours outreach work every week by the North Lambeth and North Southwark Community Education Project. This Project has also helped fund the Group's three publications to date.

STEPNEY BOOKS
19 Tomlins Grove, London E3   01-790-6420

A community publishing group.

TOLLCROSS WRITERS' WORKSHOP
Riddle's Court, 322 Lawnmarket, Edinburgh EH1 2PG   031-226-3456

The group was formed in May 1980, with the involvement of the WEA Industrial Branch and Tutor Organiser, and meets fortnightly. Its membership is 25 in total, and attendance at meetings averages 18 people or so, ranging in age from 15 to 68; 2/3 of the group are male. Publications include *Clockwork* – stories and poems by workshop members, of which the 750 print run has sold out – forthcoming publications are *Clockwork 2* and *With Foot in Mouth* by Jacqueline Robertson. Members of the group are drawn from the Tollcross locality, but also from other housing schemes and inner city areas throughout Edinburgh. The group does local public readings in the area and elsewhere. Until recently the workshop had no external financial support, but now they have a co-ordinator who is paid by Lothian Region Community Education Department.

The workshop's concerns are principally with content rather than style, with a strong emphasis on mutual support in writing about difficult personal experiences. Half the members are unemployed and there is an overlap with a WEA Unemployed Workers' Course.

TOTTENHAM WRITERS' WORKSHOP
Drayton Community Centre, Gladesmore Rd, London N15

The workshop began as a Workers' Educational Association class in Autumn 1979, meeting weekly. It now meets fortnightly, with an average attendance of 6-10, people of widely assorted ages, mostly women. It has published two anthologies, largely self-financed, but with some help for the second one from the Local Arts Council. It meets in a Community Centre and has given public performances there and (more usually) in pubs – sometimes in conjunction with other writers' workshops.

TOWER HAMLETS WORKER WRITERS' GROUP
178 Whitechapel Rd, London E1   01-247-0216

The group formed in late 1978. It meets fortnightly, usually attracting between 8 and 12 people to the meetings. For a long time the group was mainly male, but is now about equal as between men and women. Age ranges from late teens to middle age. All the members live in Tower Hamlets. Two publications so far: *No Dawn in Poplar* and *Poetry and Prose Calendar 1982*. Both are published by the Tower Hamlets Arts Project (THAP), which also provides funds for the group. The group has read its work at pubs and festivals, and also at TEEF (the yearly The East End Festival) at the Half Moon Theatre.

VOICES
61 Bloom Street, Manchester M1 3LY   061-236-2773

Voices contains short stories, poems, autobiography, cartoons, lino-cuts, photographs, as well as the latest news on working class literature.

Voices started in 1971 as a group of Manchester trade unionists with an interest in literature. The Federation of Worker Writers was formed in 1976 by groups involved in community publishing. In 1980 *Voices* became the Federation's official magazine.

Voices is the only regular national publication of working-class writing.

Voices sees itself as continuing in the tradition of *The Ragged Trousered Philanthropist*, but also reflecting the very different world of today, in which writing by women and black writers has a special place.

Voices is also of interest to librarians and teachers of English, Literacy and General Studies, who may wish to introduce learning materials more closely related to the backgrounds of their students.

Voices welcomes subscriptions and mail orders from individuals and libraries.

Voices also welcomes standing orders from trade union district and regional committees, Co-op member relations committees and other such organisations.

Voices is sold in most alternative and socialist bookshops. Where there is no section for people's history and culture, we sometimes get shelved under poetry. £2.50 for four issues. 75p for single copies including back numbers.

WOMEN AND WORDS
137 Newton Rd, Sparkhill, Birmingham   021-733-6063

Women and Words was started in the belief that many women write – poems, stories, diaries, fragments about our lives – but that this writing is often kept secret and looked on with embarrassment by the women who do it. From its beginnings as a WEA class in February 1980 it has developed into a contact point for about forty women writers, of all ages and with various occupations. We meet on Tuesdays, the original group in the evening and a new group in the daytime with a creche: at a typical meeting there will be about ten women, but the number varies between five and fifteen. We have published one anthology, *Don't Come Looking Here*, and a second is due out in Spring 1982. Both have been made possible by loans from the WEA, but after more than a year during which that body paid tutor fees it has now had to withdraw this support and our funding is now limited to the payment of administrative expenses, partly by the WEA and partly by a local adult education project. We have given several public readings, in pubs, at women's and other festivals, on women's studies courses, and, most enjoyably, with other women's writing groups, particularly Home Truths in Manchester.

WORD AND ACTION PUBLICATIONS
23 Beaucroft Lane, Colehill, Wimbourne, Dorset   0202-883197

Word and Action (Dorset) Ltd was started in 1972 in Dorset as a community theatre and publications cooperative.

We grew out of the nationwide movement in Community Arts which challenged the outdated belief that culture is the property of a highly educated minority, to be found only in the theatres, art centres and museums of our larger cities; or between the glossy covers of an expensively promoted book.

As a result our publications are concerned with developing the particular artistic character of our region.

Word and Action's approach to writing is one of acceptance rather than criticism. We do not aim to provide expert advice for aspiring professional writers, but to encourage ordinary people to write as freely and honestly as possible.

Word and Action (Dorset) Ltd. is a non-profit distributing cooperative subsidised by the Arts Council of Great Britain.

We have published a series of books of local poetry, and are now working on local history and autobiography.

WRITE FIRST TIME
Westbourne Road Centre, Westbourne Rd, Bedford MK40 1JD
0234-64454

A quarterly newspaper/magazine bringing together writing and recordings by adult 'literacy students' across the country.

Further reading

For a full listing of the work available from the various member groups of the FWWCP see the Federation's *Publications List 1981/2* – available (price 50p inc. postage) from FWWCP c/o 10 Brief St, London SE5.
    We offer here a short list of other relevant publications.

1. *Writing* published by FWWCP, 1978.
2. *The Politics of Literacy*, (ed) Martin Hoyles. Writers & Readers Publishing Co-op.
3. *Silences* by Tillie Olsen. Virago.
4. *Man Made Language* by Dale Spender. RKP.
5. *Education & the Labour Movement* by Brian Simons. Lawrence & Wishart.
6. *The Long Revolution* and *The Country & the City* by Raymond Williams. Penguin.
7. *People's History & Socialist Theory* (ed) Raphael Samuels. RKP.
8. *In and against the State* London/Edinburgh Weekend Return Group. Pluto.
9. *The Making of the English Working Class* by E.P. Thompson. Penguin.
10. *The Ragged Trousered Philanthropist* by Robert Tressell. Panther.

Note: The history of working class writers and readers, from the 17th to the 20th century, is still largely unexplored. That work which has been done is often only published in learned journals, or is published only in America, or is out of print. We thought it best only to list books which are actually in print and available fairly easily from bookshops and libraries. No general or comprehensive study of this area has been published since R.D. Altick's *The English Common Reader* (1957), and that excellent book has itself been out of print for years. There is still a long silence to be broken in this particular field of history and literary studies.

Afterword

The initiative for this book came from the Minority Press Group (now Comedia). It is part of a series dealing with various aspects of cultural production in contemporary British society: newspapers, magazines, community papers, the women's press, radio, television, as well as other forms of popular communication. Since it has always been a feature of the books produced within the FWWCP to explain concisely how they came to be produced, by whom and in what ways, we feel that this book should be no exception.

In the autumn of 1980, Dave Morley of the MPG approached Ken Worpole, who was treasurer of the FWWCP and one of its founding members, suggesting that the MPG would like to commission and help facilitate the production of such a book. Some twenty people active within the Federation, or who had been involved in some kind of related work, were invited to a meeting to discuss the writing of such a book. The first meeting was held at the Centerprise bookshop and community centre in London on 13th December 1980 and such was the enthusiasm for the project that work began immediately. A list of topics to be covered was drawn up and various people volunteered to produce first drafts of sections on these topics. The meetings were tape-recorded and Dave Morley, on behalf of MPG, transcribed the tapes to produce minutes of the meetings and acted as secretary and convenor for the group.

In the following months different sections of the book were drafted by Stephen Yeo and Paddy Maguire (QueenSpark, Brighton); Roger Mills (THAP Community Bookshop, E. London); Rebecca O'Rourke ('Women and Words', Birmingham); Sue Shrapnel (Centerprise and *Write First Time*, E. London). Gerry Gregory, who was unable to attend any of the meetings, sent in a list of themes which he had drawn up based on his extensive reading of Federation books. Philip Corrigan (Institute of Education) also attended meetings and commented on the draft manuscripts. Barbara Shane, Chairperson of the FWWCP, Mike Kearney, the ex-full-time co-ordinator of the FWWCP and Ken

Worpole, treasurer of the FWWCP, attended the meetings and fed in experiences of their own involvement in the Federation.

In November of 1980 Ken Worpole produced a first draft of the whole book from the various partial drafts. This was sufficiently monolithic to set people to work again to revise all sections so that they should reflect the actual difficulties and problems of all the issues raised. This was done in a six week period over Christmas of 1981. A two day meeting in early January 1982 involved the reading aloud of most of the new drafts, agreeing amendments and finally leaving the tidying up to the two co-ordinating editors: Dave Morley and Ken Worpole. It was a very time-consuming process, occasionally hot-tempered, but finally brought together with genuine solidarity. It is not a seamless text but then it couldn't be, since it reflects the individual styles and 'truths' of a number of individual activists, who, whilst certainly in broad political agreement, are bound to reflect differences of detail. (After all, socialism is as much about differences as it is about sameness of things). Neither is it the definitive understanding of the subject some of us dreamed it might be. But it is, we hope, a fairly thoughtful understanding of a movement *in movement* and we hope of use to those who read it.

In mid-February 1982 it was handed over to an outside sub-editor to tidy up incongruities of style, repetitions and unintended obscurities. From that point on MPG handled the type-setting, printing and publishing and distribution processes. The two people who took responsibility for editing the book were paid for the labour. Everyone else involved in the project worked voluntarily, receiving only travel expenses. The readers, we hope, will now make their contribution. We would welcome feedback from readers – suggestions and criticisms. That way everyone moves on one stage further... for arguments about culture class and political commitment are not just about where we come from, but very much about where we are going to.

Comedia Publishing Group
9 Poland St, London W1

Comedia Publishing produces books on all aspects of the media including: the press and publishing; TV, radio and film; and the impact of new communications technology.

The Comedia publishing series is based on contemporary research of relevance to media and communications studies courses, though it is also aimed at general readers, activists and specialists in the field.

The series is exceptional because it spans the media from the mainstream and commercial to the oppositional, radical and ephemeral.

New titles

No. 9. **Nukespeak – The media and the bomb**
Edited by Crispen Aubrey

Nukespeak is the official language of nuclear war, presented to us by the military and political propagandists.

Nukespeak looks at how and why media coverage of the nuclear issue varies, at examples of censorship, at how the jargon obscures the truth, at how journalists approach the subject and what practical steps are open to disarmament groups to press their case. A useful and controversial intervention in the current debate about whether Britain should give up its bomb.

paperback £2.50 hardback £7.50

No. 8. **NOT the BBC/IBA – The case for community radio**
by Simon Partridge

The rise of the community politics and media movements has rekindled interest in a new form of local radio.

The book describes the existing BBC and IBA structures and makes the case for a much more local democratic and accountable system, where there is far more scope for audience involvement. It describes how the idea came about and examples of how it can work both at home and abroad.

Part 2 is a comprehensive guide of how to put the idea into practice.

paperback £1.95 hardback £5.00